AAT

External Auditing

Level 4

Professional Diploma in
Accounting

Question Bank

For assessments from
September 2017

Second edition 2017

ISBN 9781 5097 1266 3

British Library Cataloguing-in-Publication Data

A catalogue record for this book is available
from the British Library

Published by

BPP Learning Media Ltd
BPP House, Aldine Place
142-144 Uxbridge Road
London W12 8AA

www.bpp.com/learningmedia

Printed in the United Kingdom

Your learning materials, published by
BPP Learning Media Ltd, are printed on
paper obtained from traceable
sustainable sources.

We are grateful to the AAT for permission to reproduce
the sample assessment(s). The answers to the sample
assessment(s) have been published by the AAT. All other
answers have been prepared by BPP Learning Media Ltd.

BPP Learning Media is grateful to the IASB for permission
to reproduce extracts from the International Financial
Reporting Standards including all International Accounting
Standards, SIC and IFRIC Interpretations (the Standards).
The Standards together with their accompanying
documents are issued by:

The International Accounting Standards Board (IASB) 30
Cannon Street, London, EC4M 6XH, United Kingdom.
Email: info@ifrs.org Web: www.ifrs.org

Disclaimer: The IASB, the International Financial
Reporting Standards (IFRS) Foundation, the authors and
the publishers do not accept responsibility for any loss
caused by acting or refraining from acting in reliance on
the material in this publication, whether such loss is
caused by negligence or otherwise to the maximum extent
permitted by law.

BPP
LEARNING MEDIA

Contents

BPP LEARNING MEDIA

Introduction

This is BPP Learning Media's AAT Question Bank for *External Auditing*. It is part of a suite of ground-breaking resources produced by BPP Learning Media for AAT assessments.

This Question Bank has been written in conjunction with the BPP Course Book, and has been carefully designed to enable students to practise all of the learning outcomes and assessment criteria for the units that make up *External Auditing*. It is fully up to date as at June 2017 and reflects both the AAT's qualification specification and the sample assessment provided by the AAT.

This Question Bank contains these key features:

- Tasks corresponding to each chapter of the Course Book. Some tasks are designed for learning purposes, others are of assessment standard

- AAT's AQ2016 sample assessment 1 and answers for *External Auditing* and further BPP practice assessments

The emphasis in all tasks and assessments is on the practical application of the skills acquired.

Approaching the assessment

When you sit the assessment it is very important that you follow the on screen instructions. This means you need to carefully read the instructions, both on the introduction screens and during specific tasks.

When you access the assessment you should be presented with an introductory screen with information similar to that shown below (reproduced from the *External Auditing* sample assessment).

We have provided this **sample assessment** to help you familiarise yourself with our e-assessment environment. It is designed to demonstrate as many of the question types that you may find in a live assessment as possible. It is not designed to be used on its own to determine whether you are ready for a live assessment.

At the end of this sample assessment you will receive an immediate assessment result. This will only take into account your responses to tasks 1–17, 20, 21 and 23 as there are elements of the assessment that are computer marked. In the live assessment, your responses to tasks 18, 19 and 22 will be human marked.

You have **2 hours** to complete this assessment.

This assessment contains **23 tasks** and you should attempt to complete **every** task. Each task is independent. You will not need to refer to your answers to previous tasks. Read every task carefully to make sure you understand what is required.

Where the date is relevant, it is given in the task data. Both minus signs and brackets can be used to indicate negative numbers **unless** task instructions say otherwise.

You must use a full stop to indicate a decimal point. For example, write 100.57 NOT 100,57 OR 100 57.

You may use a comma to indicate a number in the thousands, but you don't have to. For example, 10000 and 10,000 are both acceptable.

The actual instructions will vary depending on the subject you are studying for. It is very important you read the instructions on the introductory screen and apply them in the assessment. You don't want to lose marks when you know the correct answer just because you have not entered it in the right format.

In general, the rules set out in the AAT sample assessments for the subject you are studying for will apply in the real assessment, but you should carefully read the information on this screen again in the real assessment, just to make sure.

A full stop is needed to indicate a decimal point. We would recommend using minus signs to indicate negative numbers and leaving out the comma signs to indicate thousands, as this results in a lower number of key strokes and less margin for error when working under time pressure. Having said that, you can use

whatever is easiest for you as long as you operate within the rules set out for your particular assessment.

You have to show competence throughout the assessment and you should therefore complete all of the tasks. Don't leave questions unanswered.

In some assessments, written tasks may be human marked. In this case you are given a blank space or table to enter your answer into. You are told in the assessments which tasks these are.

When asked to fill in tables, or gaps, never leave any blank even if you are unsure of the answer. Fill in your best estimate.

Finally, take note of any task specific instructions once you are in the assessment. For example you may be asked to enter a date in a certain format or to enter a number to a certain number of decimal places.

Grading

To achieve the qualification and to be awarded a grade, you must pass all the mandatory unit assessments, all optional unit assessments (where applicable) and the synoptic assessment.

The AAT Level 4 Professional Diploma in Accounting will be awarded a grade. This grade will be based on performance across the qualification. Unit assessments and synoptic assessments are not individually graded. These assessments are given a mark that is used in calculating the overall grade.

How overall grade is determined

You will be awarded an overall qualification grade (Distinction, Merit, and Pass). If you do not achieve the qualification you will not receive a qualification certificate, and the grade will be shown as unclassified.

The marks of each assessment will be converted into a percentage mark and rounded up or down to the nearest whole number. This percentage mark is then weighted according to the weighting of the unit assessment or synoptic assessment within the qualification. The resulting weighted assessment percentages are combined to arrive at a percentage mark for the whole qualification.

Grade definition	Percentage threshold
Distinction	90–100%
Merit	80–89%
Pass	70–79%
Unclassified	0–69% Or failure to pass one or more assessment/s

Re-sits

The AAT Professional Diploma in Accounting is not subject to re-sit restrictions.

You should only be entered for an assessment when you are well prepared and you expect to pass the assessment.

AAT qualifications

The material in this book may support the following AAT qualifications:

AAT Professional Diploma in Accounting Level 4, AAT Professional Diploma in Accounting at SCQF Level 8 and Certificate: Accounting (Level 5 AATSA).

Supplements

From time to time we may need to publish supplementary materials to one of our titles. This can be for a variety of reasons. From a small change in the AAT unit guidance to new legislation coming into effect between editions.

You should check our supplements page regularly for anything that may affect your learning materials. All supplements are available free of charge on our supplements page on our website at:

www.bpp.com/learning-media/about/students

Improving material and removing errors

There is a constant need to update and enhance our study materials in line with both regulatory changes and new insights into the assessments.

From our team of authors BPP appoints a subject expert to update and improve these materials for each new edition.

Their updated draft is subsequently technically checked by another author and from time to time non-technically checked by a proof reader.

We are very keen to remove as many numerical errors and narrative typos as we can but given the volume of detailed information being changed in a short space of time we know that a few errors will sometimes get through our net.

We apologise in advance for any inconvenience that an error might cause. We continue to look for new ways to improve these study materials and would welcome your suggestions. If you have any comments about this book, please email nisarahmed@bpp.com or write to Nisar Ahmed, AAT Head of Programme, BPP Learning Media Ltd, BPP House, Aldine Place, London W12 8AA.

Question Bank

Chapter 1 – Principles of auditing and professional ethics

Task 1.1

There are two types of assurance engagement which a practitioner is permitted to perform – a reasonable assurance engagement and a limited assurance engagement.

Identify which type of assurance engagement an external audit is by selecting the appropriate option.

An external audit conducted under the International Standards on Auditing is:

▾

Picklist:

A limited assurance engagement
A reasonable assurance engagement

Task 1.2

You have started work for a company that is in the process of being audited for the first time. The directors have heard that the auditors do not certify that the accounts are correct but instead speak of obtaining reasonable assurance and eventually expressing an opinion on the truth and fairness of the financial statements.

Select which concept relates to each statement.

The auditor does not examine each and every transaction in detail to ensure that it is correctly recorded and properly presented.	▾
The view given in the financial statements is based on a combination of both fact and judgement and therefore cannot be characterised as either 'absolute' or 'correct'.	▾
The financial statements should comply with relevant standards to ensure that they are not biased in any way.	▾

Picklist:

Fairness
Reasonable assurance
Truth

Task 1.3

Which ONE of the following records is a business entity registered as a company not required to keep?

	✓
Records of money spent and received by the company from day to day and what the money related to (sales, purchases and wages)	
Returns from customers and suppliers	
Details of the assets and liabilities of the company	
Statements of stock (inventory) held at the financial year end	

Task 1.4

Registered companies must have an audit.

Complete the following statement on what an audit is by filling in the gaps.

An audit is an [▼] by an [▼] [▼] examiner to ensure that the [▼] of a company, prepared from the accounting records by the [▼] give a of [▼] the company's affairs and transactions in the year.

Picklist:

Assurance
Auditors
Balances
Correct
Directors
Examination
Financial statements
Independent
Qualified
Statement of financial position
True and fair view

Task 1.5

Select whether the following statements in respect of who is exempt from the requirement to have an audit are true or false.

Private companies with a turnover of less than £10.2 million, assets of less than £5.1 million and less than 50 employees on average throughout two years are exempt from the requirement to have an audit.	▼
Public companies with a turnover of less than £10.2 million and assets of less than £5.1 million are exempt from the requirement to have an audit.	▼
All companies for whom it has been unnecessary to record a transaction in the financial year are exempt from the requirement to have an audit.	▼

Picklist:

True
False

....

Task 1.6

Select whether the following statements in respect of the requirement to keep accounting records are true or false by ticking the appropriate column.

	True ✓	False ✓
Companies must keep accounting records that are sufficient to disclose with complete accuracy at all times, the financial position of the company.		
Companies must keep accounting records that are sufficient to disclose with reasonable accuracy at the company's accounting year end, the financial position of the company.		
Companies must keep accounting records that are sufficient to disclose with reasonable accuracy at all times the financial position of the company.		

....

BPP
LEARNING MEDIA

Task 1.7

For the last few years your firm has helped Celina, a sole trader, prepare her accounts for HM Revenue and Customs. Celina is about to incorporate her business and has asked for your advice on the advantages to the company of having its accounts audited (you may assume that the company would be able to claim exemption from audit).

Required

Set out the advantages of an audit for the benefit of Celina.

Task 1.8

Select whether the following statements in respect of the Financial Reporting Council are true or false.

The Financial Reporting Council (FRC) is an independent body that issues professional guidance for auditors to follow.	▼
The Government has delegated responsibility for standard setting and monitoring to the FRC.	▼
Auditors in the UK are required to follow the professional standards issued by the FRC.	▼
Global standards for auditors are issued by the International Auditing and Ethical Standards Board (IAESB).	▼

Picklist:

True
False

Task 1.9

Select whether the following statements in respect of the role of the International Audit and Assurance Standards Board (IAASB) are true or false.

IAASB is committed to producing high quality audit standards and promoting international convergence in auditing practice.	▼
IAASB is a constituent body of the FRC, which is the independent regulator of accounting and auditing in the UK.	▼
When IAASB prepares new standards, it first researches the standard and drafts it, then subjects it to public comment, before issuing it after approval from 51% of the board.	▼

Picklist:

True
False

Task 1.10

Select which one of the following is not a limitation of auditing by ticking the appropriate box.

	✓
The fact that the directors make subjective judgements in preparing the financial statements and there are instances where a range of values could be acceptable	
The fact that the directors might not provide the auditors with all the information they need, either intentionally or unintentionally	
The fact that fraud may be being concealed, even by falsifying documents which might reasonably appear genuine	
The fact that accounting systems are subject to human error	

Task 1.11

There is a difference between an auditor's legal relationship with the company being audited and other stakeholders.

Select the appropriate duty of care in each situation below.

The company being audited.	▼
Individual shareholders in the company being audited.	▼
The bank of the company being audited, who has given the company a substantial overdraft facility.	▼

Picklist:

Duty of care cannot exist
Duty of care is automatic
Duty of care must be proved

Task 1.12

Auditors may use various methods of limiting their personal liability to clients.

Select the appropriate liability limitation method in each situation.

A contract stating the maximum sum an auditor is liable for, or the maximum proportion of liability an auditor will accept responsibility for.	▼
A legal entity which bears some similarity to a company and gives similar legal protection to members in respect of liability.	▼
Payments made to a third party to ensure a pay out to injured parties in the event of a negligence claim being successful.	▼

Picklist:

Liability limitation agreement
Limited liability partnership
Professional indemnity insurance

Task 1.13

Attendance at inventory count is an accepted procedure for establishing the existence of inventories. Owing to pressure of work, you neglected to arrange for the physical observation of inventory at the premises of Leesmoor Ltd at 31 March 20X4, but your review of the instructions indicated that company procedures appeared to be in order. You decided to accept the amount at which inventory was stated in the financial statements at 31 March 20X4 on the grounds that:

(a)   The instructions appeared to be satisfactory

(b)   No problems had arisen in determining physical inventory quantities in previous years, and

(c)   The figures in the financial statements generally 'made sense'.

You issued your unmodified audit report on 28 May 20X4 and without your knowledge or consent, Leesmoor used the financial statements and the auditor's report to obtain a material unsecured long-term loan from a third party. In October 20X4 the company was forced into liquidation and the long-term loan holder lost the amount of his loan. During the liquidation proceedings it became clear that inventory quantities at 31 March 20X4 had been considerably overstated.

Required

Set out the probable legal position of your firm in respect of the above matter commenting specifically on the following:

(a)   The possibility of demonstrating your firm was negligent.

(b)   The fact that the inventory figure in the financial statements apparently 'made sense'.

(c)   The fact that you were not informed that the financial statements and your audit report were to be used to obtain additional finance.

Task 1.14

You are the auditor of a premiership football club of which you are also a fan. You have applied for a season ticket but there is a three-year waiting list.

One of the directors suggests that he can help you to jump the queue and if you make out a cheque for the season ticket, he will sort out a seat for you in the directors' box in time for the next home game.

Select the appropriate action.

The appropriate action is…	▼

Picklist:

accept the director's offer.
decline the director's offer.

··

Task 1.15

Identify, from the picklist below, the fundamental ethical principle represented by each of the following actions taken by three audit firm employees.

The audit manager informs her employer that she has inherited a substantial number of shares in a current audit client.	▼
The audit manager decides to temporarily step down from a bank audit until he receives training on new accounting standards relevant to financial instruments.	▼
The audit senior decides to stop reviewing a client's working papers on the train when a member of the public starts sitting in the seat beside him.	▼

Picklist:

Confidentiality
Integrity
Objectivity
Professional behaviour
Professional competence and due care

··

Task 1.16

Identify, from the picklist below, the ethical threat described by each of the following situations.

DS Ltd is an audit client of your firm and its fees make up over 25% of the firm's income.	▼
MF Ltd has informed your firm that it intends to seek alternative auditors unless the proposed audit opinion delivered by your firm is changed.	▼
A new audit senior is to be assigned to the audit of JK Ltd having just previously worked as chief accountant for JK Ltd.	▼

Picklist:

Advocacy
Familiarity
Intimidation
Self-interest
Self-review

Task 1.17

Identify, from the picklist below, the most appropriate ethical safeguard for the following situations.

The audit partner has been in charge of the same audit engagement for 17 years.	▼
The audit manager is being interviewed for the vacant post of financial controller at one of his audit clients.	▼
The auditor has calculated a tax figure for use in the client's financial statements.	▼

Picklist:

Independent review of working papers

Procedures for monitoring and managing the reliance on revenue received from a single client

Rotation of senior personnel

The use of different personnel with different reporting lines for the provision of non-assurance services to an audited entity

Task 1.18

You are the audit senior on the audit of Dowhop Limited, which will be commencing shortly. Your audit assistant is David Devley, who is new to the firm and has little experience of auditing. The owner of Dowhop Limited has discussed with the audit partner the possibility that she will seek to sell the business in the near future. No one else at the company is aware of her plans. Your firm currently audits one of Dowhop's main competitors, Lindybug Limited.

The audit manager has asked that you explain some fundamental aspects of auditing to David.

Required

Compile brief notes for David's benefit explaining the following matters:

(a) **The auditor's duty of confidentiality.**

(b) **How the audit team should treat the information about the owner's intentions when it attends the client to conduct the audit.**

(c) **The issues associated with auditing both Dowhop and Lindybug.**

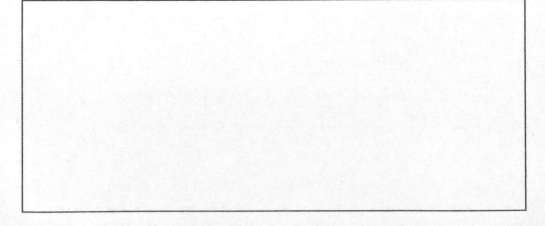

Task 2.1

Select whether the following statements in respect of the control environment are true or false.

The control environment is the attitudes, awareness and actions of management and those charged with governance about internal control and its importance.	▼
If the directors follow control activities themselves and encourage others to do so, if they promote an attitude in a company that internal control is important, and encourage staff to monitor their own performance and the performance of others in observing control, then they can contribute to an excellent control environment.	▼
If directors override controls set up in a company and give other staff the impression that controls are not important, then they will be strongly contributing to a good control environment.	▼

Picklist:

True
False

Task 2.2

An information system is an infrastructure which carries information for a company and compiles a body of information from individual pieces of information. For example, a sales invoice is entered into the information system and is converted into information about overall sales for the month or the year.

Select which is the type of information system described.

An information system that is heavily documented in physical ledgers.	▾
A system which is retained predominantly in electronic format.	▾

Picklist:

Computerised

Manual

....

Task 2.3

Control activities are the policies and procedures that help ensure that management directives about internal control are carried out. They are often simply referred to as 'controls'.

Select the type of control activity described.

A company will not place an order for goods until a senior member of staff has confirmed that order.	▾
A company locks the storeroom so that raw materials cannot be accessed.	▾
An accounts department is organised so that Debbie is in charge of invoicing and Phil is in charge of receipts.	▾

Picklist:

Information processing

Performance reviews

Physical controls

Segregation of duties

....

Task 2.4

An external auditor is required to obtain an understanding of the control environment within an audited entity.

Identify whether the following factors contribute to a strong control environment or a weak control environment by selecting the appropriate option.

	Strong ✓	Weak ✓
Directors document control policies and procedures and communicate them to all staff.		
Directors demand staff push themselves to obtain goals and promote the concept of 'by any means possible'.		
A director has perpetrated a fraud.		

Task 2.5

Which ONE of the following is not an inherent limitation of an internal control system?

	✓
Employees may make mistakes implementing controls.	
Controls may have been badly designed by management.	
Employees and third parties may collude to circumvent controls.	
Controls may be too expensive to operate on a daily basis.	

Task 2.6

All control systems are subject to limitations, hence the auditor cannot rely solely on controls testing.

Identify the type of limitation described in each statement by selecting the appropriate option.

The payroll clerk and the human resources manager, who authorises the payroll on a monthly basis, are working together to defraud the company by benefiting from the salaries of two false employees.	▼
Sales made to Dixie, a major customer, are always processed at a special discount not recognised by the computer controls, so the sales director always has to process Dixie's sales, and 'fix' the problem.	▼

Picklist:

Collusion
Human error
Management override

Task 2.7

Accounting systems have control objectives and control procedures to mitigate the risks that the control objective is not met.

Identify whether each of the following is a control objective, risk, or control procedure in respect of a sales system by selecting the appropriate option.

Customers do not pay for the goods.	▼
Customers should pay promptly for goods.	▼
Customers are allocated credit limits.	▼

Picklist:

Control objective
Control procedure
Risk

Task 2.8

Accounting systems have control objectives and control procedures to mitigate the risks that the control objective is not met.

Identify whether each of the following is a control objective, risk, or control procedure in respect of a sales system by selecting the appropriate option.

A company intends to invoice all despatches correctly.	▼
A company can match despatch records with invoices prior to invoices being sent out.	▼
A company can send out goods and not invoice them.	▼

Picklist:

Control objective
Control procedure
Risk

Task 2.9

Accounting systems have control objectives and control procedures to mitigate the risks that the control objective is not met.

Identify whether each of the following is a control objective, risk, or control procedure in respect of a purchases system by selecting the appropriate option.

A company pays for goods it has not received.	▼
A company only accepts goods it has ordered.	▼
A company compares invoices to purchase orders and GRNs.	▼

Picklist:

Control objective
Control procedure
Risk

Task 2.10

You have begun the audit of Glad Rags Limited, a textiles company. Review the information given about the purchases and payables system given below.

Accounting systems information – Glad Rags Limited

Purchases

The company keeps basic inventories of all the fabric and threads required to manufacture goods from their catalogue. When inventories fall to a certain level, the store manager requisitions a pre-set amount of that inventory. There are certain fabrics that are only used for a limited number of inventories. That fabric will only be re-ordered if a sales order is placed for items requiring the fabric.

When the purchases department receive a requisition, they place the order with the approved supplier at a prearranged price. An order document is written out and kept in the orders pending file.

When the fabric or thread is received, the store manager ensures that the quality is suitable and checks the goods against the order. The order is then passed to the accounts department and placed in the pending invoices file.

When the invoice is received, the accounts assistant, Beth Simpkins, checks the invoices against the order to ensure the price and quantity are correct and checks the VAT has been calculated correctly. She initials the invoices to show that these checks have been carried out and gives the invoice a sequence number. The invoice is then entered into the purchase ledger on the computer.

Beth prepares cheques for payment at the end of each two weeks and passes them to the director, Gladys Barton, for signature and approval. The invoices are included with the cheques as evidence of the debt.

Most suppliers send statements at the end of the month which Beth reconciles to the purchase ledger balances. The purchase ledger control account is agreed to the total of the purchase ledger balances at the end of the month.

Required

Identify the control procedures that are present in Glad Rags' system.

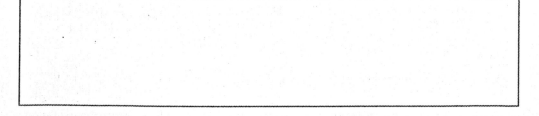

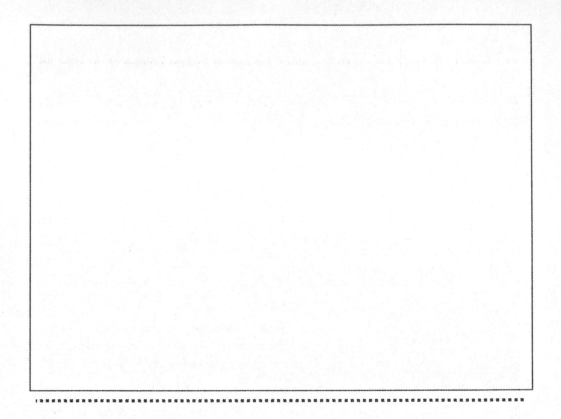

Task 2.11

Accounting systems have control objectives and control procedures to mitigate the risks that the control objective is not met.

Identify whether each of the following is a control objective, risk, or control procedure in respect of a purchases system by selecting the appropriate option.

A company wants to pay the right amount for goods purchased.		▼
A company reconciles supplier statements to the purchase ledger.		▼
A company may pay for goods which are used for personal purposes.		▼

Picklist:

Control objective
Control procedure
Risk

Task 2.12

Accounting systems have control objectives and control procedures to mitigate the risks that the control objective is not met.

Identify whether each of the following is a control objective, risk, or control procedure in respect of a wages system by selecting the appropriate option.

The company should pay employees for work done.	▾
The company could make incorrect payments to HMRC.	▾
The company reviews payroll against budgets.	▾

Picklist:

Control objective
Control procedure
Risk

Task 2.13

Accounting systems have control objectives and control procedures to mitigate the risks that the control objective is not met.

Identify whether each of the following is a control objective, risk, or control procedure in respect of a capital expenditure system by selecting the appropriate option.

The company buys assets it does not need.	▾
Depreciation rates should reflect the useful life of an asset.	▾
The company keeps a non-current assets register.	▾

Picklist:

Control objective
Control procedure
Risk

Task 2.14

Accounting systems have control objectives and control procedures to mitigate the risks that the control objective is not met.

Identify whether each of the following is a control objective, risk, or control procedure in respect of a purchases system by selecting the appropriate option.

Goods inwards are checked and recorded.	▾
Goods may be used for personal gain.	▾
Goods are available when required for use in the business.	▾

Picklist:

Control objective
Control procedure
Risk

Task 2.15

Which ONE of the following methods are auditors unlikely to use to record company systems?

	✓
A graph	
A flowchart	
Narrative notes	
A questionnaire	

Task 2.16

Complete the definition below.

A walkthrough test is a test designed to ensure that the system [▾] as the [▾] have been told that it does. They select a transaction in a particular area (for example, a sale or a purchase) and trace it through the company's information system from the initial point (for example, the sales [▾] or the purchase [▾]).

Picklist:

Auditors
Directors
Goods received note
Ledger
Operates
Order
Requisition
Staff
Supplier statement

Task 2.17

> **Accounting system information**
>
> *Sales revenue*
>
> The company manufactures clothes to order from a catalogue.
>
> When an order is received, the sales department checks that the customer has not exceeded their credit limit and then issues a two-part order document. The sales department fill in the appropriate values for the order. One copy is sent to the production department for the order to be completed and the other is filed alphabetically in the customer file in the sales department.
>
> Once the order is completed, two-part despatch notes are raised. When the factory manager, Ian Jones, has checked the order, one copy of the despatch note is despatched with the goods (to be signed and returned), and one part is matched to the production department's sales order and sent to accounts to raise the invoice. Jane Hill raises the invoices from the order and despatch note, enters them on the computer and sends them out to customers.
>
> Most customers pay in around 60 days. Cheques are passed to Beth Simpkins, one of the accounts assistants, when they come in and she updates the cashbook and the sales ledger. Cheques are banked twice a week. Cheques are kept securely in the safe until banking.
>
> Jane sends out statements to customers each month. Glad Rags' customers are mostly all reputable high street stores and there are rarely irrecoverable debts.

Required

Use the accounting system information for sales at Glad Rags Limited given above to complete the internal control questionnaire also given below.

Internal control questionnaire – revenue and receivables system

Question	Yes/No	Comment
Are orders only accepted from low credit risks?		
Are despatches checked by appropriate personnel?		
Are goods sent out recorded?		
Are customers required to give evidence of receipt of goods?		
Are invoices checked to despatch notes and invoices?		
Are invoices prepared using authorised prices?		
Are invoices checked to ensure they add up correctly?		
Are sales receipts matched with invoices?		
Are statements sent out regularly?		
Are overdue accounts reviewed regularly?		
Are there safeguards over post received to ensure that cheques are not intercepted?		
Are bankings made daily?		
Would it be appropriate to perform tests of control in this area? (Give reason/reasons in the comments box.)		

BPP LEARNING MEDIA

Task 2.18

The external auditor may seek to place reliance on internal controls in order to restrict substantive testing.

In each of the following circumstances identify whether the external auditor is likely to place reliance or place no reliance on controls by selecting the appropriate option.

	Reliance ✓	No reliance ✓
A company where there is an internal audit function which monitors controls on a systematic and regular basis.		
A small company where the owner-manager has virtual control over all accounting transactions, aided by his part-time, unqualified wife.		

Task 2.19

An external auditor is required to obtain an understanding of the control environment within an audited entity.

Identify whether the following factors contribute to a strong control environment or a weak control environment by selecting the appropriate option.

Management communicate controls values to staff and ensure new staff are thoroughly training in controls procedures.	▼
Management emphasise the importance of targets over procedures.	▼
Management include adherence to company procedures in annual appraisals for staff members.	▼

Picklist:

Strong
Weak

Task 2.20

The following are descriptions of procedures within the sales system of a company.

Identify whether each procedure indicates a strength or a deficiency in the system by selecting the appropriate option.

	Strength ✓	Deficiency ✓
Julie raises the sales invoices on the basis of the goods received notes she is sent by the warehouse. She inputs the information, prints the invoices, and sends them out. No other procedures are carried out.		
Statements are sent to customers on a monthly basis.		

Task 2.21

The following are descriptions of procedures within the purchases system of Kingsley Ltd.

For each procedure, state whether it indicates a strength or a deficiency in the system.

Sandra reconciles supplier statements with the purchase ledger as she receives them.	▼
Payments, which are approved by a director, are made on a monthly basis on the basis of a printout of due items from the purchase ledger.	▼

Picklist:

Deficiency
Strength

Task 2.22

The following are descriptions of procedures within the payroll system of Weasley Ltd.

Identify whether each procedure indicates a strength or a deficiency in the system by selecting the appropriate option.

Each member of staff is allocated a personnel file on arrival, which is updated for any changes in pay rates or hours.	▼
The payroll is created by the wages clerk on the last Thursday of a month. She runs the payroll package which automatically produces a bank payments list and notifies the bank to pay the salaries.	▼

Picklist:

Deficiency
Strength

Task 2.23

The following are descriptions of procedures within the non-current assets system of Primrose Ltd.

For each procedure, identify whether it indicates a strength or a deficiency in the system by selecting the appropriate option.

	Strength ✓	Deficiency ✓
The company maintains a non-current asset register. The operations manager checks the register to physical assets once a year.		
The operations manager and the purchasing director meet monthly to discuss asset requirements for the business.		

Task 2.24

The following are descriptions of procedures within the inventory system of Calend Ltd.

For each procedure, identify whether it indicates a strength or a deficiency in the system by selecting the appropriate option.

Inventory is kept in a locked store, secured by the key card system in operation at the company. All members of staff are issued with key cards.	▼
The production manager reviews levels of inventory and makes requisitions on a monthly basis.	▼

Picklist:

Deficiency
Strength

Task 2.25

An entity uses internal control procedures in order to mitigate the risks to which the entity is exposed. Listed below are two internal control procedures which are applicable to an entity's sales system.

Match each risk mitigated to the internal control procedure by completing the table with the appropriate risk for the procedure.

Internal control procedure	Risk mitigated
Credit checks are run on new customers.	▼
Despatches are checked for quality before leaving the warehouse.	▼

Picklist:

Customers are invoiced incorrectly.
Customers are issued credit notes incorrectly.
Customers are not good credit risks.
Customers don't pay promptly.

Task 2.26

An entity uses internal control procedures in order to mitigate the risks to which the entity is exposed. Listed below are two risks which are applicable to an entity's purchases system.

Match each risk mitigated to the internal control procedure by completing the table with the appropriate procedure for the risk.

Risk	Internal control procedure to mitigate
Company pays for poor quality goods	▼
Company pays for the same invoice twice	▼

Picklist:

Company only purchases from approved suppliers
Company provides supporting evidence of payments before approval
Company records payments promptly on the purchases ledger
Company reviews all goods inwards for condition

Chapter 3 – Obtaining audit evidence

Task 3.1

Identify whether the following statements concerning evidence are true or false by selecting the appropriate option

An auditor needs to obtain sufficient, appropriate evidence.		▼
Sufficient means evidence from at least two sources.		▼

Picklist:

True
False

....

Task 3.2

Auditors use tests of controls and substantive procedures to gather audit evidence.

For each of the procedures below, identify whether it is a test of control or a substantive procedure.

	Test of control ✓	Substantive procedure ✓
Observation of inventory count		
Inspection of invoices to vouch cost of new non-current assets		
Recalculation of depreciation charge		

....

Task 3.3

Auditors use tests of controls and substantive procedures to gather audit evidence.

For each of the procedures below, identify whether it is a test of control or substantive procedure.

	Test of control ✓	Substantive procedure ✓
A test to verify the operation of procedures designed to safeguard the business		
A comparison of financial and non-financial information by the auditor		
A test to verify an assertion made in the financial statements		

Task 3.4

The following is a list of controls in the system at Daredevil Ltd.

Identify how an auditor would test these controls by matching the control with the relevant test. If necessary, you can use the same answer twice. Some controls may require two tests.

Controls	Tests of control
The company has a policy for choosing suppliers.	▼
Goods received are examined for quantity and quality.	▼
Goods received are checked against the order.	▼

Picklist:

Observe the accounts assistant checking supplier invoices
Observe the store manager receiving some goods
Review a sample of orders
Scrutinise paid invoices
Scrutinise reconciliations

Task 3.5

The following is a list of controls in the system at Daredevil Ltd.

Identify how an auditor would best test these controls, by matching each control with the tests below. (Some answers may be used more than once.)

Controls	Tests of control
Hours worked are recorded.	▼
Hours worked are reviewed.	▼
Payroll is prepared by a director.	▼

Picklist:

Observe staff arriving at work
Observe the director preparing payroll
Review clockcards
Review payroll

Task 3.6

You are planning the audit of Glad Rags Limited. Materiality has been set at £70,000.

Required

Using the extracts from the statement of financial position below, select which of the items listed below is likely to be subject to mainly analytical procedures or tests of detail.

STATEMENT OF FINANCIAL POSITION FOR GLAD RAGS LIMITED

Year ended 30 November 20X4

	20X4		20X3	
	£	£	£	£
Non-current assets		21,940		24,794
Current assets				
Inventory	352,599		302,214	
Receivables	1,345,933		1,412,911	
Bank	29,583	1,728,115	23,491	1,738,616
Net current assets		1,750,055		1,763,410
Payables: amounts falling due within one year		(365,038)		(355,893)
		1,385,017		1,407,517

Non-current assets	▼
Inventory	▼
Receivables	▼
Bank	▼
Payables	▼

Picklist:

Analytical procedures
Tests of details

....

Task 3.7

The accountant at Forsythe Limited has presented you with a draft statement of financial position for the year, which is given below. The audit manager has suggested that it is likely that materiality will be set at £65,000.

Draft statement of financial position for Forsythe Ltd year ended 31 December 20X4

	20X4 £	20X4 £	20X3 £	20X3 £
Non-current assets		3,812,594		3,862,591
Current assets				
Inventory	423,781		405,863	
Receivables	10,020		9,930	
Bank balance			25,795	
		433,801		441,588
Current liabilities				
Bank overdraft	(17,000)			
Trade payables	(226,313)		(220,879)	
Accruals	(32,476)		(29,583)	
Bank loan	(100,000)		(100,000)	
		(375,789)		(350,462)
Long term liabilities				
Bank loan		(2,425,000)		(2,525,000)
		1,445,606		1,428,717

Required

Select which balances below should be tested in detail and which should be reviewed using analytical procedures.

Non-current assets	▼
Inventory	▼
Receivables	▼
Bank	▼
Trade payables	▼
Accruals	▼
Bank loan	▼

Picklist:

Analytical procedures
Tests of details

Task 3.8

As part of verification techniques in respect of repairs and maintenance expense, the auditor inspects invoices. The auditor will gain assurance about different assertions depending on the information on the invoice.

In respect of the information below, identify the assertion for which that information will provide assurance by selecting the appropriate option.

Description on the invoice	▼
Date on the invoice	▼

Picklist:

Accuracy
Classification
Cut off

Task 3.9

Two types of computer-assisted audit techniques (CAAT) are test data and audit software.

For each of the procedures listed below, select the type of CAAT which would be used to perform that procedure.

Selection of a sample of sales ledger accounts over £30,000		▼
Input of sales invoices with false customer numbers to ensure application controls function correctly		▼
Analytical procedures on statement of profit or loss, on a line by line approach		▼

Picklist:

Audit software
Test data

Task 3.10

Identify whether the following statements concerning selecting items for testing are true or false by selecting the appropriate option.

When sampling, the auditor must ensure that all sampling items have an equal chance of selection.		▼
When an auditor selects a sample of invoices at random from the filed invoices for the year, this is known as the random approach to sampling.		▼

Picklist:

True
False

Task 3.11

When selecting items in order to perform tests of controls, the auditor has to consider a number of factors.

For each of the following factors, identify whether they will result in an increase or decrease in sample size by selecting the appropriate option.

	Effect on sample size
The auditor intends to increase his reliance on tests of controls.	▼
The auditor is selecting a sample of sales invoices, when a new customer means the volume of sales at the client has increased by 20%.	▼
The auditors' tolerable deviation rate rises from 1.5% to 2%.	▼

Picklist:

Increase
Decrease
No effect

Task 3.12

The objective of a substantive test will determine the population from which the sample for testing is selected.

For each of the objectives set out below, match the population from which the sample should be selected.

Obtain evidence of the completeness of the trade payables balance	▼
Obtain evidence that the bank balance is fairly stated	▼

Picklist:

Bank letter
Bank reconciliation
Bank statement
Cash book
Purchase invoice
Purchase ledger
Purchase requisition

Task 3.13

Once auditors have assessed control risk, they choose an overall approach to the audit.

Identify whether the following statements about audit approach are true or false by selecting the appropriate option.

	True ✓	False ✓
The auditor may take a combined approach, where he will test controls and then reduce his subsequent substantive testing (although he must always carry out tests of detail on material items).		
The auditor may take a substantive approach, where he does not test controls, but instead renders control risk as high and conducts more tests of detail instead.		

Task 3.14

The external auditor may seek to place reliance on internal controls in order to restrict substantive testing.

For each of the following circumstances, identify the most likely approach to be adopted by the external auditor by selecting the appropriate option.

	Reliance ✓	No reliance ✓
The directors of LightLynx Ltd demand close attention to control procedures, and they monitor how the system is operating on a monthly basis.		
At Simlaglow Ltd, there is an accounting staff of two, the financial controller, and his assistant.		
There are ten people in the accounts department at Luxicon Ltd. The financial controller keeps a close interest in all transactions, and often intervenes to speed up proceedings.		

Task 3.15

Complete the table below. In the left-hand column you should list the financial statement assertions and in the right-hand column give an example of a test that fulfils each assertion.

Financial statement assertion	Example test

Chapter 4 – Planning: Audit risk

Task 4.1

Identify whether the following statements in respect of obtaining an understanding of the business are true or false by selecting the appropriate option.

Auditors are required to obtain an understanding of the entity and its environment only when the client is a new client.		▼
Auditors are required to obtain an understanding of the entity and its environment so that they are able to assess the risks relating to the audit.		▼

Picklist:

True
False

Task 4.2

Complete the following statements about audit risk.

Audit risk is the risk that the auditors give an inappropriate opinion on the financial statements. It is made up of three components:

- [▼] risk – the risk arising as a result of the nature of the business, its transactions and environment.

- [▼] risk – the risk that the control system at the company does not detect, correct or prevent misstatements.

  (These two risks combined are the risk that misstatements will exist in the financial statements in the first place.)

- [▼] risk – the risk that auditors do not discover misstatements in the financial statements.

Picklist:

Accounts
Audit
Business
Control
Detection
Human
Inherent

Task 4.3

The auditor takes a number of steps after gaining an understanding of a client and its environment.

Which ONE of the following steps would NOT be taken?

	✓
Identify inherent and control risks while obtaining an understanding of the entity	
Relate identified risks to what could go wrong at a financial statement level	
Consider if the risks could cause material misstatement	
Identify detection risk as part of a review of audit firm procedure	

Task 4.4

Set out what can go wrong with balances, transactions and events at a financial statement level.

Task 4.5

The external auditor is required to undertake analytical procedures as part of the planning process in order to identify the risk of misstatement of figures in the financial statements. The results of some analytical procedures carried out on sales are listed below.

Identify the most likely conclusion to be drawn as a result of the procedures undertaken.

Sales revenue has increased by 3% but the gross profit margin is down by 1.5%.	▼
Sales in the last month of the year were 5% higher than in previous years, and also 4% higher than the average for a month for the company.	▼

Picklist:

More information required to draw a conclusion
Sales revenue may be overstated
Sales revenue may be understated

Task 4.6

Green Valley Limited is a company owning three garden centres, one of which has a cafe. You have the following information about Green Valley's sales from the prior year audit file:

Sales income	Shop 1	Shop 2	Shop 3	Café
April – July	Average 400 customers per day @ £30			
Feb/March Aug/Sept	Average 300 customers per day @ £20	Average 75% of income of shop 1	Average 65% of income of shop 1	Average ½ customers of shop 1 per day @ £8
Oct – Jan	Average 200 customers per day @ £15			

Perform analytical procedures on this information and select whether the sales income figures below might be under or overstated or appear reasonable.

Shop 1 sales income is £2,521,634.	▼
Cafe sales income is £431,996.	▼
Total sales income is £5,673,676.	▼

Picklist:

Appear reasonable
Overstated
Understated

....

Task 4.7

Listed below are two risks that the auditors have noted at Linklynx Ltd.

Identify what could go wrong at a financial statement level in each situation by selecting the appropriate option.

The company issues inventory to customers on a sale or return basis.	▼
The non-current asset register is not reconciled regularly with the actual assets.	▼

Picklist:

Assets could be over- or understated
Assets could be overstated
Assets could be understated

....

Task 4.8

When planning an audit of financial statements, the external auditor is required to consider how factors such as the entity's operating environment and its system of internal control affect the risk of misstatement in the financial statements.

Identify whether the following factors are likely to increase or reduce the risk of misstatement.

	Increase ✓	Reduce ✓
The company operates in a highly regulated industry.		
The company has an internal audit function committed to monitoring internal controls.		
The company has set ambitious growth targets for all its salesmen, to be judged at the end of the financial year.		

Task 4.9

The external auditor assesses control risk in order to determine the audit approach.

Identify whether the following factors are likely to lead to the auditor assessing that there is an increase or decrease in control risk.

	Increase ✓	Decrease ✓
The role of sales ledger clerk has been filled by four different people during the year, following the retirement of a long-standing sales ledger clerk at the end of last year.		
The financial controller is a qualified accountant, as are two of his high level staff.		
The directors have a positive attitude towards controls and enforce them company-wide.		

Task 4.10

Complete the following sentences.

A control such as a [▼] may [▼] unauthorised access to a computer programme so that errors cannot be deliberately input.

Alternatively a control such as a reconciliation [▼] mistakes, which the person carrying out the reconciliation can then [▼], so that there is no misstatement in the financial statements as a result.

Picklist:

Correct
Detects
Password
Prevent
Reconciliation
Reject

....

Task 4.11

Identify whether the following statements about materiality are true or false by selecting the appropriate option.

	True ✓	False ✓
Materiality is the concept of importance to users.		
It is relevant to auditors because they will only test items which are material.		
Calculating materiality and selecting samples on the basis of materiality helps the auditor to reduce audit risk to an acceptable level.		

....

Task 4.12

Which ONE of the following does not suggest a significant risk?

	✓
A risk of fraud	
A complex transaction	
A significant transaction with a related party	
A transaction in the normal course of business for the entity	

Task 4.13

Complete the definition.

Material and pervasive is taken to mean that the misstatement is:

- [　　　　▼] to one item in the financial statements.

- [　　　　▼] to one item, but the item could represent a substantial portion of the financial statements.

- If relating to a disclosure, [　　　　▼] to users' understanding of the financial statements.

Picklist:

Confined
Fundamental
Important
Judgemental
Not confined

Chapter 5 – Planning: Audit procedures

Task 5.1

Background information

Glad Rags Limited is a private company set up by Bill and Gladys Burton 50 years ago. It manufactures clothes which it sells mainly to high street clothing stores. The company relies heavily on two major customers: British Clothes Stores (BCS) and Value Mart (VM). The company has another 20 customers on the sales ledger, but BCS and VM account for 60% of revenue. BCS have recently told Gladys that they are auditing their suppliers to ensure that the suppliers meet their stringent quality requirements. Glad Rags has three major suppliers (Fine Fabrics, The Fabric Wholesaler and Terry's Threads).

The company is 100% owned by Gladys Burton, who inherited her husband's shares when he died in 20X0. She is the sole director. Gladys has no children to inherit the business and has confided to the auditors that she is thinking of selling the business in the near future. Her plans are not known to any other members of staff at Glad Rags.

Your audit firm has been the auditor for five years. The firm has always found Gladys to be honest and reliable. Gladys has a key role in the day to day running of the business. She oversees the production of the company sales catalogue, runs the personnel department (hiring and firing staff and dealing with the payroll) and determines which suppliers the company will use.

Revenue is £7 million with gross profit at 30% and profit for the year of 9.5%.

Gladys employs a part-time bookkeeper (Bill Overton) to oversee the two accounts assistants (Jane and Beth) and to produce monthly and annual accounts. Including these staff members and Gladys, there are eight administrative staff and 50 machinists/cutters.

Materiality has been set at £70,000 for this year's audit.

Required

Using the background information given, identify two areas of risk for the audit of Glad Rags Limited, explaining why they are risks. You should also set out what could go wrong at a financial statement level in respect of each risk.

Task 5.2

Which ONE of the following audit procedures is NOT a test of completeness of non-current assets?

	✓
Obtain a summary of non-current assets and reconcile with the opening position (additions and disposals)	
Compare non-current assets in the general ledger with the non-current asset register and obtain explanations for any differences	
Inspect assets to see if they are in use and good condition	
Check that assets which physically exist are included in the register	

Task 5.3

Identify the assertion at which each of the following audit procedures are directed by selecting the appropriate option.

Review depreciation rates for reasonableness (given asset lives, residual values, replacement policy, possible obsolescence)		▼
Vouch title deeds of buildings		▼
Inspect a sample of assets listed in the non-current assets register		▼

Picklist:

Accuracy, valuation and allocation
Existence
Rights and obligations

Task 5.4

It is 10 November 20X3 and you have been asked to work on the audit of the non-current asset section of the accounts of Kandistors Limited for the year ended 31 December 20X3. The company manufactures sweets and chocolate which it sells and delivers to the retail trade.

The partner in charge of the audit has asked you to examine the non-current assets section of the company's most recent management accounts. The company maintains a non-current assets register and you should assume that there will be no non-current asset acquisitions between the dates of 1 November 20X3 and 31 December 20X3.

Required

Set out, in a manner suitable for inclusion in an audit plan, TEN audit procedures to be carried out to meet the following assertions:

(a) **Completeness**
(b) **Existence**
(c) **Rights and obligations**
(d) **Accuracy, valuation and allocation**

You are not required to consider disposals of non-current assets or depreciation charges.

For each procedure mentioned in your plan, where appropriate, you should identify the associated assertion.

Task 5.5

Below is a schedule of non-current assets at Craftys Limited. The opening figures have already been verified to the prior year audit file and financial statements.

	Land £	Buildings £	Vehicles £	Fittings £	Total £
Cost at 1 January 20X4	1,500,000	2,750,000	128,970	121,173	4,500,143
Additions			42,000	697	42,697
Cost at 31 December 20X4	1,500,000	2,750,000	170,970	121,870	4,542,840
Accumulated depreciation at 1 January 20X4		503,000	66,893	67,659	637,552
Depreciation		55,000	25,646	12,048	92,694
Accumulated depreciation at 31 December 20X4		558,000	92,539	79,707	730,246
Carrying amount at 1 January 20X4	1,500,000	2,247,000	62,077	53,514	3,862,591
Carrying amount at 31 December 20X4	1,500,000	2,192,000	78,431	42,163	3,812,594

Depreciation rates:

Buildings – 2% straight line
Vehicles – 15% straight line
Fittings – 10% straight line

Required

Set out, in a matter suitable for inclusion in an audit plan, the procedures that should be done to verify that the non-current assets figure in the financial statements is true and fair.

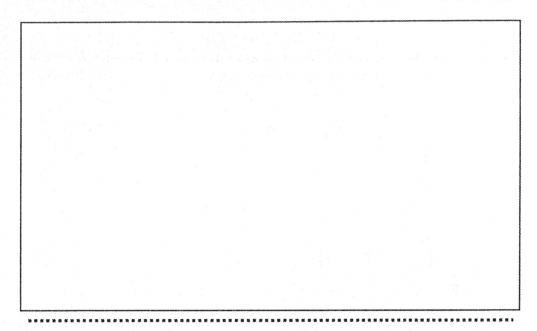

Task 5.6

As part of your work on non-current assets, you have reviewed the repairs and maintenance expense code. You have found the following material items there:

Repair to main jigsaw	£24,000
Replacement engine	£25,000
Maintenance contract with Micheals	£12,000
New computer software for sales	£8,000

By how much should additions to non-current assets be increased?

	✓
£69,000	
£57,000	
£33,000	
£25,000	

Task 5.7

Which ONE of the following company controls is a key factor in auditing whether the inventories in the financial statements actually exist?

	✓
The inventory count	
Inventory records	
The locked stores	
The reorder levels	

Task 5.8

Match the following situations with their effect on the financial statements by completing the table.

The company records a sale but the inventory is also counted as existing at the year end.	(a) (b)
The company accept goods on the day of the inventory count, which get included in the count, but do not record the invoice in purchases until the following year.	(a) (b)

Picklist:

Assets are overstated
Assets are understated
Liabilities are overstated
Liabilities are understated
Profit is overstated
Profit is understated

Task 5.9

When auditing the value of finished goods, set out what components of cost auditors will need to verify, and what evidence they will seek in respect of those components.

Task 5.10

Which ONE of the following tests does NOT contribute to the auditors' assurance that net realisable value of inventory is higher than cost?

	✓
Ensuring inventory which appeared damaged at the inventory count has been valued accordingly	
Examine sales prices after the year end to ensure that none have significantly dropped (perhaps to below cost)	
Review quantities of inventory sold after the year end to ensure that goods are not obsolete	
Review sales prices during the year to ensure that none have been significantly low	

Task 5.11

You are going to attend the annual inventory count at Glad Rags Limited. Last year's working papers show that the major items in inventories were standard white thread (code: S01) and cotton jersey fabric in black and blue (codes: CJ02 and CJ03). The sample size for test counts was 12.

MEMO

From: Joe Worple, Store Manager, Glad Rags Limited

To: Audit senior

I enclose the instructions for this year's inventory count, which will take place at 3pm on 30 November. The machines will not be operating during the count. Ten machinists have volunteered to be counters, the rest have accepted a half-day.

There are no new issues relating to inventory this year, except that the company has just bought a large consignment of specialist fabric A001 to service a large order for Value Mart. The reorder levels for most of the standard fabrics have not changed from last year. In December, we shall be starting some major orders for clients for the spring season, so we have a high level of inventory as usual. As you know, our fabric and threads are measured in metres and the bales are marked up with lengths removed. We do not remeasure every bale of fabric.

Most of the fabric and threads are in the stores. The machinists will be asked to finish work in progress at the end of the day before the count. There will be some goods awaiting delivery which are kept in the machining room. We are not planning to make any deliveries on the day of the count and have requested that our suppliers do not make deliveries on the day.

Glad Rags Limited

Inventory count instructions 30 November 20X4

Overseer – Joe Worple, Store Manager

Checkers – Betty Fradin, Liz Tyler, Mandeep Singh, Bet King, Elspeth Worthing, Jill Manson, Jane Smith, Bev Jones, Claire King, Ann Jones

All pieces should be finished before the count commences. Machinists should not commence new pieces after 2pm. All finished goods need to be placed in the east end of the machine room to be counted.

Checkers should work in pairs and will be allocated to different areas of the stores. Two checkers will count finished goods in the machine room. Each checker will be issued with a sheet stating the fabrics and threads in their section which they must count. One checker should check the amounts of each fabric and write them down on the sheet.

Once a bale has been counted, it must be marked with a red sticker to show that it has been counted. The second checker should check the first checker's work. When an item has been checked for a second time, it should be marked with a green sticker. Joe Worple will carry out random checks on completed inventory sheets to ensure that items have been checked correctly.

Each checking pair should remeasure four bales of fabric to ensure that the record attached to the bale is correct.

No checker must leave until permitted by Joe Worple. Checkers will be paid £6 an hour for the count, which must be noted and authorised by Joe Worple.

Required

Using the information given:

(a) **Set out the key issues at the inventory count.**

(b) **Appraise the count instructions provided by the company and conclude whether you believe the count will be capable of producing a reliable figure for the existence of inventory.**

Task 5.12

Here is a working paper showing the test carried out on inventory cut off. Materiality is £70,000.

Client:	Glad Rags Ltd		Prepared by:	J Devoran
Accounting date:	30 November 20X4		Date:	2 January 20X5
			Reviewed by:	
			Date:	

Inventory cut off

Last deliveries out

Sales order/GDN	Customer	Agreed to November Sales Day Book
200894/DN12403	Value Mart	✓
200895/DN12404	BCS	✓
200896/DN12405	Tisco Stores	✓

The above items have all been excluded from the inventory count

Last deliveries in (from invoices pending file – these were the only three orders received pending invoices)

Order	Supplier	Agreed to November Purchase Day Book
P1013	Fine Fabrics Ltd	✓
P1017	Fine Fabrics Ltd	✓
P1021	Terry's Threads	*

* This invoice was not received until 15 December and was included in December's Purchase Day Book. The value was £2,476.

All the above items were included in the inventory count.

Identify the appropriate conclusion to draw about inventory cut off at this stage by selecting the appropriate option.   ▼

Picklist:

Cut off is fairly stated
Further work is required before a conclusion can be drawn

Task 5.13

Below are the results of the testing carried out at the inventory count of Glad Rags Limited:

Client:	Glad Rags Ltd	Prepared by:	J Devoran
Accounting date:	30 November 20X4	Date:	30 November 20X4
		Reviewed by:	
		Date:	

Inventory existence

Items remeasured

Inventory code	Amount per record	Amount measured	Correct
C01	20.75m	20.75m	Yes
L02	13.45m	13.45m	Yes
S03	2.5m	2.5m	Yes
CJ04	16.75m	16.75m	Yes
CJ05	2.35m	2.35m	Yes

Arithmetical accuracy of records

Inventory code	Record adds?
L01	Yes
L03	Yes
S05	Yes

Conclusion – controls over inventory measurement operate effectively

Test counts

Inventory code	Amount per sheet Inventory	Amount physically present	Count correct?
A001	200m	200m	Yes
S01	4 × 50m	4 × 50m	Yes
	1 × 21m	1 × 21m	
CJ02	2 × 50m	2 × 50m	Yes
	1 × 1.35m	1 × 1.35m	
CJ03	2 × 50m	2 × 50m	Yes
	1 × 25.50m	1 × 25.50m	
CJ04	16.75m	16.75m	Yes
S02	4 × 50m	4 × 50m	Yes
	1 × .25m	1 × .25m	
L04	12m	12m	Yes
N01	135m	135m	Yes
N02	127m	127m	Yes
X101 White t-shirts	250	250	Yes
X103 Blue t-shirts	175	175	Yes
Z111 Babygros	1,000	1,000	Yes

Conclusion – test counts indicate count operated efficiently

Identify which of the tests needs to be carried out to draw a conclusion as to whether the existence of inventory is fairly stated by selecting the appropriate option. ▼

Picklist:

Trace test count items to final inventory sheets
Trace test count items to purchase invoices

Task 5.14

Grols Ltd designs, prints and configures paper and cardboard packaging to order for customers. It has a large inventory of raw material, work in progress and finished goods. Batches of raw material are indistinguishable, and they are kept on large shelves, and reordered when a reorder limit is reached. The company has experienced the following two problems:

(1) A hole in the factory roof which resulted in a leak in the raw material stores.

(2) The financial difficulties of a major customer, to whom the most recent consignment has not been shipped.

Required

Set out, in a manner suitable for inclusion in the audit plan:

(a) The audit risks relating to inventory.

(b) The procedures to be undertaken in order to ensure that inventory valuation is fairly stated in the financial statements.

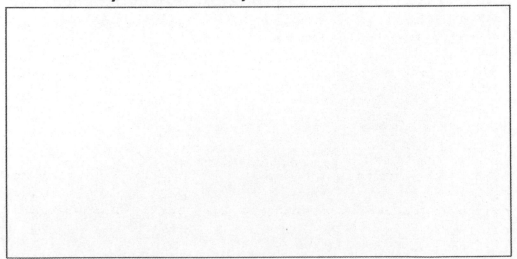

Task 5.15

Below are the last goods recorded in and out of the factory on the last day of the financial year (31 December). The invoices in respect of these have been traced to the ledgers.

Last goods in		Traced to
X13639443		December purchase ledger
R0204863		January purchase ledger
Last goods out		
FG135933 – Careys		December sales ledger
FG135934 – Seepe		January sales ledger

Which ONE of the following options shows the item(s) on which cut off is correct?

	✓
X13639443 only	
FG135933 and X1369443 only	
R0204863 and FG135934 only	
FG135934 only	

Task 5.16

Masterful Ltd operates a perpetual inventory system. The year end is 31 December. Inventory is counted four times a year, in February, May, August and October. The company has a sophisticated computerised system which can identify the value of inventory on hand at any time. The system produces goods in and out notes when inventory comes in or out of the factory, those notes are matched with invoices in the accounts department.

Required

Set out, in a manner suitable for inclusion in the audit plan the procedures to be undertaken in order to ensure that the existence and completeness of inventory is fairly stated in the financial statements.

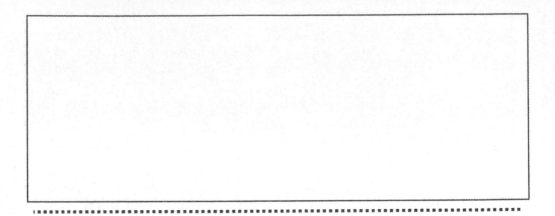

....

Task 5.17

Which of the following balances must an auditor NOT neglect when selecting a sample for auditing receivables?

(i)   Material balances
(ii)   Old unpaid accounts
(iii)   Credit balances
(iv)   Zero balances
(v)   Accounts which have been paid by the date of examination

	✓
(i) only	
(i) and (ii) only	
(i), (ii), (iii) and (iv) only	
All of them	

....

Task 5.18

An audit junior will carry out the audit work on valuation of debts of Glad Rags. An aged trade receivables analysis from the sales ledger at 30 November 20X4 will be available. Glad Rags' standard credit terms are 60 days.

Required

Set out, in a manner suitable for inclusion in an audit plan, the procedures to be performed on the receivables valuation.

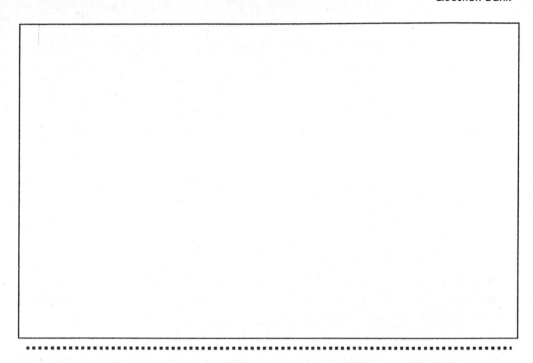

Task 5.19

During the last quarter of year ended 31 December 20X9, Carl Ltd starting supplying a new customer, Diversity Ltd. Carl Ltd had carried out initial credit checks before accepting orders from this customer then began to supply Diversity Ltd goods on standard credit terms of 60 days. The audit is being planned during the last week in December, at which time, Diversity Ltd has not paid any of its balance. Carl Ltd has requested that the auditors do not seek to confirm the balance directly with Diversity, as it is a new customer, and the credit controller does not want to appear to be being heavy handed at the outset of the relationship. The balance at 31 December is material.

Diversity is a relatively new company which has grown exponentially in its field in the first year of business, raising questions in the financial press about its ability to maintain functioning working capital.

Required

Set out, in a manner suitable for inclusion in the audit plan:

(a) The audit risks relating to this receivable balance.

(b) The procedures to be undertaken to ensure that it is fairly stated in the financial statements.

Task 5.20

You are continuing your work at Glad Rags Limited. The following is a working paper, showing work done on the receivables balance.

Client:	Glad Rags Ltd	Prepared by:	A Student
Accounting date:	30 November 20X4	Date:	19 January 20X5
		Reviewed by:	
		Date:	

Receivables circularisation

Objective: To ensure that receivables exist and are genuine obligations to the company

Work done: Replies reconciled to sales ledger balances. Where replies not available, cash received after date gives sufficient evidence concerning existence and rights.

Debtor	Balance per sales ledger £	Agreed to debtor reply	Comments/reconciliation	Balance Agreed?
BCS	484,536	No	Difference is a receipt for £44,938	o/s
Brodies	74,973	Yes	–	Yes
Tisco Stores	78,805	No	Difference is requested credit for damaged goods returned.	o/s
Value Mart	323,024	Yes	–	Yes
Cavanaghs	14,388	Yes	–	Yes
H and T	18,933	N/A	Balance agreed to cash receipts in Dec and Jan total £18,933	Yes
Nice Clothes	17,231	N/A	Balance agreed to cash receipts in Dec and Jan total £17,231	Yes
Value Clothes	22,315	Yes	–	Yes

Required

Identify which of Glad Rags Limited's accounting records each of the reconciling items should be checked to, by matching the record with each reconciling item.

(a)   **BCS difference**

(b)   **Tisco stores difference**

Picklist:

Bank statements
Post year end sales ledger
Pre year end sales ledger
Goods received note
Goods returned note

Task 5.21

In relation to bank letters, complete the statements below.

Bank letter requests should be made by the ...	▼
Bank letter requests should be sent to the bank ...	▼

Picklist: (Bank letter requests should be made by the ...)

auditors.
directors.

Picklist: (Bank letter requests should be sent to the bank ...)

a month after the year end.
a month before the year end.
at the year end.

Task 5.22

Complete the following definition, relevant to the audit of bank.

[▼] is the practice of manipulating when cash receipts and payments are recorded and sent out to manipulate the [▼] results at the year end.

For example, if a company wanted liabilities to look [▼] then it might record a number of payments (which would also therefore be included on the bank reconciliation, reducing the bank balance) but not physically send those cheques out until after the year end, so that in practice, the bank balance is [▼] than it appears to be in the accounts, as is the [▼] balance.

Picklist:

Higher
Lower
Money laundering
Payables
Receivables
Statement of financial position
Statement of profit or loss
Window dressing

Task 5.23

This is the bank reconciliation at 31 December 20X4 for a company you are auditing. The audit junior has verified the relevant figures to the cashbook and the bank letter as shown.

BANK RECONCILIATION			
31 December 20X4			
			£
Balance per cashbook		CB	(17,000)
Less 31 Dec takings			(1,278)
Add cheque payments	003465		5,398
	003466		2,476
	003467		15,398
	003468		108
	003469		2,365
	003470		3,465
	003471		791
	003472		23
Balance per bank statement		B	11,746
Key:			
B – agreed to bank letter			
CB – agreed to cashbook			

Which source of audit evidence must the remaining figures be verified against?

	✓
Pre year end cash book	
Post year end cash book	
Pre year end bank statements	
Post year end bank statements	

Task 5.24

Which ONE of the following tests should NOT be carried out to determine the completeness of long-term liabilities?

	✓
Compare opening balances to the previous year's working papers (closing balances at the end of last year)	
Examine receipts for loan repayments	
Compare balances to the general ledger	
Review minutes and cashbook to ensure that all loans have been recorded	

Task 5.25

During the year ended 31 December 20X9, Anderson Ltd took out a bank loan which is repayable over the next five years. The terms of the loan state that there is nothing to pay for the first six months, and that then the loan will be paid off in £100 instalments on a monthly basis. The loan agreement was signed on 1 February. The audit junior has verified payments of £100 to the bank in August, September, October, November and December.

Identify the balance that should be included in the financial statements in each case by selecting the appropriate option. Interest should be ignored.

Current liabilities	▼
Non-current liabilities	▼

Picklist: (Current liabilities)

£0
£500
£1,200

Picklist: (Non-current liabilities)

£1,200
£3,700
£4,900

Task 5.26

Identify whether the following statements in respect of the audit of trade payables are true or false by selecting the appropriate option.

Supplier statements provide excellent third party evidence about trade payables.	▼
Suppliers are circularised in the same way as receivables.	▼

Picklist:

True
False

Task 5.27

Which ONE of the following statements describes a situation when auditors are more likely to circularise payables?

	✓
When internal controls over purchases are weak and the auditor suspects that the trade payables balance has been understated.	
When internal controls over purchases are strong and the auditor suspects that the trade payables balance has been understated.	
When internal controls over purchases are weak and the auditor suspects that the trade payables balance has been overstated.	
When internal controls over purchases are strong and the auditor suspects that the trade payables balance has been overstated.	

Task 5.28

For each audit test below, match the test to the audit objective.

Audit objective	Audit test
Test completeness of purchases	▼
Test understatement of payables	▼

Picklist:

Reconcile purchase ledger with bank statements
Reconcile purchase ledger with supplier statements
Trace sample of purchases from initial records to the financial statements
Trace sample of purchases from the financial statements to initial records

....

Task 5.29

During the audit of Mike's Motors Ltd, an audit junior performed a supplier statement reconciliation on a sample of trade payables balances at 31 May 20X3. Mike's Motors has good controls over goods inwards. There is some concern that Mike's Motors may be trying to reduce payables in the statement of financial position as it is trying to secure a loan. The audit junior has reconciled the balance on the purchase ledger in respect of Patel Engine Parts Ltd to the supplier statement as follows:

Patel Engine Parts Ltd

	£
Balance per supplier	37,600
Less payment not on supplier statement	5,000
Less invoice 1812 not recorded in ledger	5,400
Balance per purchase ledger	27,200

Identify which of the following accounting records each of the reconciling items must be verified to by selecting the appropriate option.

Payment not on supplier statement	▼
Invoice 1812	▼

68

Picklist: (Payment not on supplier statement)

Bank statement
Both bank statement and cash book
Cash book

Picklist: (Invoice 1812)

Both
Purchase invoice
Purchase ledger

Task 5.30

Johnny's Juices Ltd is an established juice bar which has very strong controls over its purchasing and inventory. It has two suppliers of juice, who represent 90% of the payables ledger and who do not usually send out supplier statements. The managing director, Johnny, who has a good relationship with the suppliers, requested supplier statements for the year end, to benefit his auditors, but the statements were not forthcoming. The company has an integrated computer system and can produce a high level of analysis about all aspects of operations. Your firm has audited Johnny's Juices Ltd for the last four years.

Required

Set out, in a manner suitable for inclusion in the audit plan, the audit procedures to be undertaken in order to ensure that payables are fairly stated.

Task 5.31

Identify whether the following statements in respect of auditing sales revenue are true or false.

	True ✓	False ✓
Auditors often perform analytical procedures when auditing sales revenue as there is usually a great deal of analytical information about sales revenue (for example, analyses of sales per month or per product) at a company, and sales revenue has a number of predictable relationships (with receivables, with gross margin) so it is a good balance to test by analytical procedures.		
Auditors may test understatement of sales revenue by tracing a sale from the general ledger back through the system to the sales order.		

Task 5.32

Kitchy Kabinets Ltd buys, sells and fits high quality kitchen furniture. Most of its suppliers are traditional craftsmen who do not operate the most efficient billing systems.

Required

Set out, in a manner suitable for inclusion in the audit plan:

(a) **The risk associated with purchases cut off at Kitchy Kabinets Ltd.**

(b) **The objectives of year end cut-off procedures relating to the purchases system.**

(c) **The purchases year end cut-off procedures you would carry out on the audit of Kitchy Kabinets Ltd.**

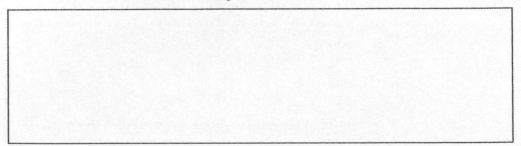

BPP
LEARNING MEDIA

Task 5.33

Which ONE of the following tests will auditors not carry out on the balance for accruals?

	✓
Recalculate the accruals	
Verify accruals by reference to previous payments	
Verify accruals by reference to subsequent payments	
Compare accruals in current statement of profit or loss and prior years	

Task 5.34

During the year, Tendosch Ltd entered into an agreement with a maintenance company to provide services to Tendosch Ltd for five years. The agreement was signed half way through the financial year. The total cost of the agreement is £60,000, with equal payments falling at the end of each year of the agreement.

Which ONE of the following balances should be included in the financial statements for the current year in respect of accruals in relation to this agreement?

	✓
£0	
£6,000	
£15,000	
£60,000	

Task 5.35

OCSL Ltd is a manufacturer of domestic cleaning machines that operates from one manufacturing site with an adjoining administrative and head office function. The cleaning machines are all sold via telephone sales with a 24 month warranty for defective goods. Due to the anti-social nature of the work, staff turnover among telephone sales operatives is high.

The auditor have decided that for the financial statements of OCSL Ltd, there are three main areas of audit risk:

(a) Warranty provisions for cleaning machinery sold to customers
(b) Payroll overpayments for staff leaving the company
(c) Prepaid telephone line rental for the sales team.

Required

Set out, in a manner suitable for inclusion in the audit plan, the audit procedures to be undertaken in order to ensure that each of the three key areas of audit risk mentioned above are fairly stated in the financial statements.

(a)   Warranty provision

(b)   Payroll overpayments

(c)   Prepaid telephone line rental

Task 5.36

SILK Ltd is a leading UK food manufacturer that supplies supermarkets and convenience stores across Europe with a variety of well-known brands. It operates several factories in major cities both in the UK and abroad, sourcing ingredients from all over Europe, and has just acquired another leading food company with manufacturing capacity in Europe. The newly acquired company also sells other well-known brands worldwide. It is expected that the new group will continue to create innovative new products that customers will continue to buy. It is also expected that the group's factories will be reviewed to ensure the right products are being made in the right locations to match customer demand.

Your firm has just been appointed as external auditor to the expanded group and will be responsible for delivering an auditor's report on the consolidated financial statements.

Required

Identify and explain the audit risks relating to the external audit of SILK Ltd. Where possible, your answer should refer to specific items in the financial statements which may be at risk of misstatement.

Task 5.37

Golden Ltd is a travel agent which operates in the UK and sells a variety of domestic and overseas holidays and other travel packages to individual customers and companies. The company has recently been involved in two high-profile events; on a flight to a lucrative new travel destination, one of their passenger planes crashed while attempting to land, injuring several passengers and causing a diplomatic incident with the local government in the destination country. The international regulator for airline flight safety has opened an investigation into the crash and has warned Golden Ltd that it may remove its flight licence if found negligent in any way.

The second event related to the outbreak of a virus aboard one of their cruise liners, which led to significant disruption of the itinerary and many cancelled excursions. Passengers affected by the virus have blamed a lack of food hygiene for their symptoms, while those not affected have claimed for damages as their dream holiday was severely disrupted because the cruise liner was quarantined for a period of seven days to contain the virus.

These two events have been widely reported in the UK national media. A significant number of customers due to depart imminently on various long-haul trips have contacted the company's head office about their right to cancel and the safe return of the 25% deposit that the company takes when a holiday is booked.

Your firm is the external auditor of Golden Ltd and you have held this position for a number of years.

Required

Identify and explain the audit risks relating to the external audit of Golden Ltd. Where possible, your answer should refer to specific items in the financial statements which may be at risk of misstatement.

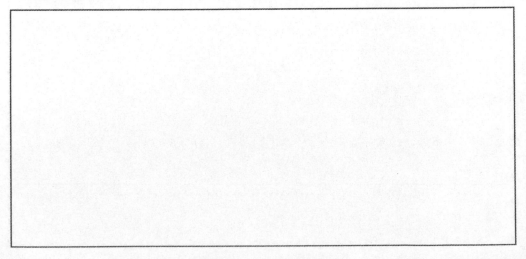

Chapter 6 – Evaluation

Task 6.1

Select whether the following statements in respect of auditors' working papers are true or false.

Working papers are prepared by the external auditor because there is a professional requirement to do so.	▼
The primary reason for recording work in working papers is so that senior staff members can review junior staff members' work.	▼
Working papers should record contentious issues and how they were resolved.	▼

Picklist:

True
False

Task 6.2

Identify whether the following statements in respect of written representations are true or false by selecting the appropriate option.

Written representations are the written evidence of everything the directors have said to auditors during the audit.	▼
Auditors are required to get written confirmation from the directors of their responsibilities with regard to the financial statements.	▼

Picklist:

True
False

Task 6.3

You are the audit senior on the audit of Dowhop Limited, which will be commencing shortly. Your audit assistant is David Devley, who is new to the firm and has little experience of auditing. The audit manager has asked that you explain some fundamental aspects of auditing to David.

Required

Compile brief notes for David's benefit explaining working papers and what they should contain.

Task 6.4

During the audit of Multicorp plc, the audit senior identified a high number of consultancy payments in the statement of profit or loss of a foreign subsidiary. On asking management to produce invoices in respect of the consultancy, management were unable to do so. Explanations as to the nature of the consultancy were sketchy. The audit senior believes that the consultancy payments represent bribes paid to government officials in the foreign country to ensure that Multicorp was able to build its factory and obtain certain licenses.

Which of the following is the correct action for the audit senior to take?

	✓
No action as such 'consultancy' is normal business practice in that country	
Report the matter to the board of directors of Multicorp	
Report the matter to the audit engagement partner	
Report the matter to the firm's Money Laundering Reporting Officer	

Task 6.5

During the external audit of Bream Ltd, the audit junior identified two instances of the sales ledger clerk allocating later receipts against earlier invoices. The instances related to the same account, and she discovered them when focusing on the receipts received in the two months after the year end.

In respect of this matter, select whether the audit junior should take no further action or refer to the supervisor.	▽

Picklist:

No further action
Refer to supervisor

Task 6.6

During the external audit of Bass Ltd, the audit junior identified three instances of sales receipts having been allocated to the wrong ledger account. The errors all occurred in August, when the sales ledger clerk was on holiday. No other such errors were found during testing.

In respect of this matter, select whether the audit junior should take no further action or refer to the supervisor.	▽

Picklist:

No further action
Refer to supervisor

Task 6.7

During the external audit of Snapper Ltd, whose year end is 31 December 20X4, the audit junior discovered, when verifying the bank statement, that many of the payments on that reconciliation did not clear the bank until near the end of January.

In respect of this matter, select whether the audit junior should take no further action or refer to the supervisor.	▼

Picklist:

No further action
Refer to supervisor

Task 6.8

During the external audit of Sturgeon Ltd, the audit junior noticed that a supplier had an incorrect VAT number. He tried the phone number on the invoice, but could not be connected. Sturgeon regularly purchases from the supplier but the total purchases are not material for the year. At the year end, the payables balance was zero.

In respect of this matter, select whether the audit junior should take no further action or should refer to the supervisor.	▼

Picklist:

No further action
Refer to supervisor

Task 6.9

ISA 265 *Communicating Deficiencies in Internal Control to Those Charged With Governance and Management* defines a significant deficiency in internal control as a deficiency or combination of deficiencies in internal control that, in the auditors professional judgement, is of sufficient importance to merit the attention of those charged with governance.

Identify whether or not the following deficiency in internal control is a significant deficiency by selecting the appropriate option:

The identification of a fraud, relating to a material monetary amount, carried out by a director of the audited entity, which was not prevented by the entity's internal control system.

▼

Picklist:

Not a significant deficiency
Significant deficiency

Task 6.10

Set out the basic elements of the standard auditor's report.

Task 6.11

Set out the four possible types of opinion in an auditor's report where there are matters that affect the auditor's opinion and explain why each would arise.

Task 6.12

The errors listed below were detected during the audit of payables at Mardens Ltd. Materiality is calculated at 5% of profit before tax. Profit before tax is £45,000. The errors below were the only errors identified during the audit:

	£
Mispostings between supplier accounts	2,439
Invoices not posted in year re goods received in year	1,029
Payment not sent out until after year end	457

Identify whether the errors must be adjusted in order to issue an unmodified audit opinion on the financial statements by selecting the appropriate option.	▼

Picklist:

Do not need to be adjusted
Must be adjusted

Task 6.13

Below are two matters which have arisen in two separate audits. Both matters are material.

Identify which audit opinion will be given in each case by selecting the appropriate option.

The directors refuse to write off a debt owed by Sandicore Ltd, a company that has gone into liquidation.	▼
The auditors believe that the company is experiencing going concern issues. The directors have failed to disclose in the financial statements, claiming their recovery plan is going to get the company back on track. The auditors have reviewed cash flow forecasts covering a period of twelve months after the end of the accounting period and believe the assumptions made were reasonable. The auditors agree that the recovery plan has a high chance of success.	▼

Picklist:

Adverse
Qualified

Task 6.14

An audit junior has calculated some financial statement ratios to see if Glad Rags Limited's financial statements appear to make sense (given below).

The key figures from the statement of profit or loss are sales revenue, which is £7,103,495, gross profit of £2,121,814 and profit for the year totalling £680,515.

Ratios		20X3
$\dfrac{\text{Gross profit}}{\text{Revenue}} \times 100$	$\dfrac{2,121,814}{7,103.495} \times 100 = 29.87\%$	(30.2%)
$\dfrac{\text{Profit for the year}}{\text{Revenue}} \times 100$	$\dfrac{680,515}{7,103,495} \times 100 = 9.58\%$	(9.52%)
$\dfrac{\text{Receivables}}{\text{Revenue}} \times 365$	$\dfrac{1,345,933}{7,103,495} \times 365 = 69 \text{ days}$	(67 days)
$\dfrac{\text{Payables}}{\text{Cost of sales}} \times 365$	$\dfrac{365,038}{4,981,681} \times 365 = 27 \text{ days}$	(28 days)

Identify whether the financial statements appear to make sense.	▼

Picklist:

Do not make sense
Make sense

Task 6.15

During the audit planning of The Glad Rags Limited, going concern was identified as a risk because:

(1) A major customer, BCS, is carrying out an audit of its suppliers.

(2) The fact that Gladys Burton, the owner-manager is considering selling the company.

Required

Set out what particular matters should be considered in carrying out a going concern review.

Task 6.16

For each of the following situations which have arisen in two unrelated audit clients, identify whether or not the audit opinion on the financial statements would be modified by selecting the appropriate option.

The auditors did not observe Handyco's inventory count at the year end, as they were not appointed until after that date. Due to the nature of the company's records, they have not been able to ascertain the existence of inventory by another method.	▼
The auditors did not observe Complicateco's inventory count due to staffing difficulties on the day. The company has detailed inventory records, and the auditors were able to attend the premises two days later and carry out test counts against the company's records. The company had maintained a record of inventory existing on the year end date and movements since are easy to trace through the system.	▼

Picklist:

Modified
Not modified

....

Task 6.17

During the audit of Daffodilly Limited, it was discovered that although the company had good controls over sales ordering and invoicing, controls over cash receipts were weak. The following deficiency was noted:

Deficiency: receipts

Post opening appears to be unsupervised and no initial list of receipts is made. Customer remittances do not appear to be retained.

Required

Prepare extracts, suitable for inclusion in a report to management of Daffodilly Limited, which set out:

(a)   The possible consequences of this deficiency, and
(b)   Recommendations you would make.

Task 6.18

During the audit of Zhong Limited, the following deficiencies in general computer controls were discovered:

- No passwords are required to access any part of the computerised accounting system.

- While security backup copies of files are taken, these copies are kept in the desk occupied by the accounts clerk.

Required

Prepare extracts, suitable for inclusion in a report to management of Zhong Limited, which set out:

(a) The possible consequences of these deficiencies, and
(b) Recommendations you would make in respect of them.

Task 6.19

During the audit of Miraglow Ltd, it was discovered that although the company maintained a central list of suppliers, the purchase team did not necessarily use it and often used different suppliers offering better prices.

Required

Prepare extracts, suitable for inclusion in a report to management of Miraglow Ltd, which set out:

(a)   The possible consequences, and

(b)   The recommendations that you would make in respect of this matter.

Task 6.20

You are the external auditor of Festival Ltd, which is a bank operating in one developed country. During your testing of the bank's payroll and human resources (HR) systems, you discovered a number of issues:

- There are no system procedures for processing new starters and leavers on the payroll.

- The HR department has experienced staffing issues which has led to payroll staff helping out with some HR duties.

- Filing within the payroll department is behind schedule and a significant number of employee records are still being processed by the HR department, despite the relevant employees having either started or left the company.

- The payroll system has been computerised during the year of audit but, due to staff shortages, was not fully tested before being implemented.

- Staff have been booked onto training courses to keep up to date with accounting for tax and other statutory deductions, but due to workload pressures, they have not been able to attend these courses.

Required

Prepare extracts, suitable for inclusion in a report to management of Festival Ltd, which set out the following in respect of the matters described above:

(a) The possible consequences, and

(b) The recommendations you would make.

Task 6.21

Jump is a leisure facility operated by a local government council on the outskirts of a large rural town. It has a swimming pool which offers lessons for children and adults as well as being open to the general public for recreational swimming. It has a gym with various fitness machines which members of the public can use either by paying a monthly subscription or on a pay-as-you-go basis. It also runs dance and fitness classes and has a cafeteria which serves food and drink. It is managed by the Head of Leisure Services who is based at the local council office in the town centre.

There is a car park at Jump that charges for parking due to its proximity to the local railway station. However, Jump does not employ any wardens to monitor parking. Cash is collected from parking machines and other tills and then returned to the general office for counting by gym instructors when they are not participating in a class. Subscriptions are also set up by gym instructors when they meet new members on their induction to the gym. Swimming lessons are paid for by direct transfers to Jump's bank account and amounts paid are reconciled by the Head of Swimming Lessons at the end of each month.

Maintenance of the fitness machines is carried out by gym instructors using information found online. The swimming pool is maintained by a retired engineer who comes in twice a week and over the weekends to monitor water purity and water usage statistics.

Accidents are logged in an accident book that requires the person's name, the date and time of their accident and any medical help administered.

Required

Prepare extracts, suitable for inclusion in a report to management of Jump, which set out the following in respect of the matters described above:

(a) The possible consequences, and
(b) The recommendations you would make.

Answer Bank

Chapter 1

Task 1.1

An external audit conducted under the International Standards on Auditing is:

A reasonable assurance engagement

Task 1.2

The auditor does not examine each and every transaction in detail to ensure that it is correctly recorded and properly presented.	Reasonable assurance
The view given in the financial statements is based on a combination of both fact and judgement and therefore cannot be characterised as either 'absolute' or 'correct'.	Reasonable assurance
The financial statements should comply with relevant standards to ensure that they are not biased in any way.	Fairness

Task 1.3

	✓
Records of money spent and received by the company from day to day and what the money related to (sales, purchases and wages)	
Returns from customers and suppliers	✓
Details of the assets and liabilities of the company	
Statements of stock (inventory) held at the financial year end	

Task 1.4

An audit is an | examination | by an | independent | | qualified | examiner to ensure that the | financial statements | of a company, prepared from the accounting records by the | directors | give a | true and fair view | of the company's affairs and transactions in the year.

Task 1.5

Private companies with a turnover of less than £10.2 million, assets of less than £5.1 million and less than 50 employees on average throughout two years are exempt from the requirement to have an audit.	True
Public companies with a turnover of less than £10.2 million and assets of less than £5.1 million are exempt from the requirement to have an audit.	False – A public company cannot qualify as small, and is therefore not exempt.
All companies for whom it has been unnecessary to record a transaction in the financial year are exempt from the requirement to have an audit.	False – Dormant companies that are a bank/insurance company or a parent in a group must still be audited.

Task 1.6

	True ✓	False ✓
Companies must keep accounting records that are sufficient to disclose with **complete** accuracy at all times, the financial position of the company.		✓ – The incorrect bits shown in bold.
Companies must keep accounting records that are sufficient to disclose with reasonable accuracy at the **company's accounting year end**, the financial position of the company.		✓ – The incorrect bits shown in bold.
Companies must keep accounting records that are sufficient to disclose with reasonable accuracy at all times the financial position of the company.	✓	

Task 1.7

The advantages of having an audit include the following:

(a)   Shareholders who are not involved in management gain reassurance from audited accounts about management's stewardship of the business.

(b)   Audited accounts are a reliable source for a fair valuation of shares in an unquoted company either for taxation or other purposes.

(c)   Some banks rely on accounts for the purposes of making loans and reviewing the value of security.

(d)   Payables and potential payables can use audited accounts to assess the potential strength of the company.

(e)   The audit provides management with an useful independent check on the accuracy of the accounting systems; the auditors can recommend improvements in those systems.

Task 1.8

The Financial Reporting Council (FRC) is an independent body that issues professional guidance for auditors to follow.	True
The Government has delegated responsibility for standard setting and monitoring to the FRC.	True
Auditors in the UK are required to follow the professional standards issued by the FRC.	True
Global standards for auditors are issued by the International Auditing and Ethical Standards Board (IAESB).	False – These standards are issued by the International Auditing and Assurance Standards Board (IAASB).

Task 1.9

IAASB is committed to producing high quality audit standards and promoting international convergence in auditing practice.	True
IAASB is a constituent body of the FRC, which is the independent regulator of accounting and auditing in the UK.	False – The FRC is the independent regulator of accounting and auditing in the UK but it is a separate entity to IAASB (their relationship is based on FRC adapting IAASB standards to the specifics of the UK accounting and auditing profession).
When IAASB prepares new standards, it first researches the standard and drafts it, then subjects it to public comment, before issuing it after approval from 51% of the board.	False – At least two thirds of members must approve it.

Task 1.10

	✓
The fact that the directors make subjective judgements in preparing the financial statements and there are instances where a range of values could be acceptable.	
The fact that the directors might not provide the auditors with all the information they need, either intentionally or unintentionally.	
The fact that fraud may be being concealed, even by falsifying documents which might reasonably appear genuine.	
The fact that accounting systems are subject to human error.	✓

This is more indicative of an inherent limitation in an internal control system.

Task 1.11

The company being audited.	Duty of care is automatic
Individual shareholders in the company being audited.	Duty of care must be proved
The bank of the company being audited, who has given the company a substantial overdraft facility.	Duty of care must be proved

Task 1.12

A contract stating the maximum sum an auditor is liable for, or the maximum proportion of liability an auditor will accept responsibility for.	Liability limitation agreement
A legal entity which bears some similarity to a company and gives similar legal protection to members in respect of liability.	Limited liability partnership
Payments made to a third party to ensure a pay out to injured parties in the event of a negligence claim being successful.	Professional indemnity insurance

Task 1.13

Auditors' liability depends on whether negligent accountants owed a duty of care to those who have relied on their accounts. If the auditors knew a third party would rely and they failed to disclaim liability, they could be found liable.

(a) The possibility of demonstrating negligence:

All FRC pronouncements and in particular auditing standards are likely to be taken into account when the adequacy of the work of auditors is being considered in a court of law or in other contested situations.

In the case of Leesmoor Ltd, the auditors did not attend to observe the company's physical inventory count procedures, which is an accepted audit practice. Whether this was negligent would depend on whether or not the auditors could satisfy the court as to whether there were good practical reasons for non-attendance and the other audit work which they carried out in relation to inventory provided sufficient appropriate audit evidence on which to base their opinion. However, this may prove to be difficult.

(b) The fact that the inventory figure in the financial statements apparently 'made sense':

This suggests that the main audit evidence on which the auditors based their opinion, in relation to the inventory figure, was the result of their analytical procedures in this area. As the auditors seem, through pressure of work, to have neglected to attend the inventory count, then one would expect them to have carried out more extensive analytical procedures than would perhaps normally have been the case for that client. If it appeared that the auditors had only carried out a minimal amount of procedures, then they would very likely be open to a charge of negligence.

(c) The fact that the auditors were not informed that the financial statements were to be used to obtain additional finance:

Past case law shows that judges do not care to attribute a duty of care to unknown third parties. It is unlikely that a judge would rule that the auditors had a duty of care to the lenders that they were unaware of, as there is no possibility that such a duty could have been implied in dealings between them.

Task 1.14

| The appropriate action is... | decline the director's offer |

Being able to jump a three-year waiting list for a football season ticket is likely to be viewed as a big favour which could compromise your independence (a likely familiarity threat). Even if you are not of the mind to give in to client pressure, the client may feel in a position to exert pressure.

Sharing an executive box with the directors on a regular basis may entail receiving a certain amount of hospitality, which increases the familiarity threat (affecting independence of mind). It may also give the wrong impression to the world in general (affecting independence in appearance).

Task 1.15

The audit manager informs her employer that she has inherited a substantial number of shares in a current audit client.	Integrity – This is due to the manager being honest about her inheritance.
The audit manager decides to temporarily step down from a bank audit until he receives training on new accounting standards relevant to financial instruments.	Professional competence and due care – It is unethical to undertake audit work without being competent.
The audit senior decides to stop reviewing a client's working papers on the train when a member of the public starts sitting in the seat beside him.	Confidentiality – The senior does not want to risk confidential information about the client becoming public.

Task 1.16

DS Ltd is an audit client of your firm and its fees make up over 25% of the firm's income.	Self-interest – This is excessive fee-dependency and is likely to lead to the firm valuing their business more than their ethics.
MF Ltd has informed your firm that it intends to seek alternative auditors unless the proposed audit opinion delivered by your firm is changed.	Intimidation – Such 'opinion shopping' represents a threat to your firm's objectivity.
A new audit senior is to be assigned to the audit of JK Ltd having just previously worked as chief accountant for JK Ltd.	Self-review – As accountant, it is likely that the new senior will probably have worked on the financial statements under audit so will be reviewing his own work.

Task 1.17

The audit partner has been in charge of the same audit engagement for 17 years.	Rotation of senior personnel – Different jurisdictions have different rules but 17 years as auditor of the same client is likely to impair your objectivity!
The audit manager is being interviewed for the vacant post of financial controller at one of his audit clients.	Independent review of working papers – It is possible that the audit manager may overlook some client errors in order to secure the job.
The auditor has calculated a tax figure for use in the client's financial statements.	The use of different personnel with different reporting lines for the provision of non-assurance services to an audited entity – This can reduce the significance of ethical threats presented by this situation.

Task 1.18

Confidentiality

The auditor has a duty to keep company affairs private. The auditor is likely to come across sensitive information when carrying out his audit and must not use that information to the advantage of a third party or to his own advantage (such as insider trading).

In certain situations the auditor will disclose confidential information about a client – this can be for any of the following reasons:

(1)   If the auditor is **permitted** to do so by the client (for example, when liaising with the previous auditor for Dowhop).

(2)   If the auditor is **obliged** to disclose information (for example, by a court requiring evidence).

(3)   If the auditor needs to **act in the public interest** (for example, when complying with a regulatory inspection of its working papers).

Information about owner's intentions

In respect of the information concerning the director's intentions to sell the business, this information will impact on certain aspects of the audit work to be undertaken. However, the auditors have a duty not to mention this to other members of staff at Dowhop and to be circumspect with the information when attending the client – for example, not leaving working papers making reference to it lying around and even being discreet if wanting to talk to the director about it.

Auditing both Dowhop and Lindybug

As both these companies are in competition with each other, the auditor may access commercially sensitive information that each might find useful about the other, so it is important for David to respect confidentiality regarding such information. In such cases, both Dowhop and Lindybug should have consented to the firm acting for them simultaneously before we accepted each engagement. We also need to be alert to any situations where we may (either deliberately or by accident) undertake actions that favour one client's interests above the other (for example, if they both requested our advice in the event of bidding for the same contract, or in the case of the owner of Dowhop attempting to sell the company to Lindybug and requesting our firm's help in securing the highest price).

Chapter 2

Task 2.1

The control environment is the attitudes, awareness and actions of management and those charged with governance about internal control and its importance.	True
If the directors follow control activities themselves and encourage others to do so, if they promote an attitude in a company that internal control is important, and encourage staff to monitor their own performance and the performance of others in observing control, then they can contribute to an excellent control environment.	True
If directors override controls set up in a company and give other staff the impression that controls are not important, then they will be strongly contributing to a good control environment.	False

Task 2.2

An information system that is heavily documented in physical ledgers.	Manual
A system which is retained predominantly in electronic format.	Computerised

Task 2.3

Control activities

A company will not place an order for goods until a senior member of staff has confirmed that order.	Information processing
A company locks the storeroom so that raw materials cannot be accessed.	Physical controls
An accounts department is organised so that Debbie is in charge of invoicing and Phil is in charge of receipts.	Segregation of duties

Task 2.4

	Strong ✓	Weak ✓
Directors document control policies and procedures and communicate them to all staff.	✓	
Directors demand staff push themselves to obtain goals and promote the concept of 'by any means possible'.		✓ – This attitude implies controls may be overridden to achieve results.
A director has perpetrated a fraud.		✓ – Control environment is about the attitudes, actions and awareness of high level staff.

Task 2.5

	✓
Employees may make mistakes implementing controls.	
Controls may have been badly designed by management.	
Employees and third parties may collude to circumvent controls.	
Controls may be too expensive to operate on a daily basis.	✓

Task 2.6

The payroll clerk and the human resources manager, who authorises the payroll on a monthly basis, are working together to defraud the company by benefiting from the salaries of two false employees.	Collusion
Sales made to Dixie, a major customer, are always processed at a special discount not recognised by the computer controls, so the sales director always has to process Dixie's sales, and 'fix' the problem.	Management override

Task 2.7

Customers do not pay for the goods.	Risk
Customers should pay promptly for goods.	Control objective
Customers are allocated credit limits.	Control procedure

Task 2.8

A company intends to invoice all despatches correctly.	Control objective
A company can match despatch records with invoices prior to invoices being sent out.	Control procedure
A company can send out goods and not invoice them.	Risk

Task 2.9

A company pays for goods it has not received.	Risk
A company only accepts goods it has ordered.	Control objective
A company compares invoices to purchase orders and GRNs.	Control procedure

Task 2.10

Controls present:

- The necessity for orders is evidenced prior to ordering and a requisition is raised.
- The company has a policy for choosing suppliers.
- Goods received are examined for quantity and quality.
- Goods received are checked against the order.
- Supplier invoices are checked to the order.
- Supplier invoices are checked for prices, quantities and calculations and given a reference number.
- Purchases are entered on the purchase ledger promptly.
- Cheque requests are presented for approval with supporting documentation.
- Supplier statements are reconciled to the purchase ledger.
- The purchase ledger control account is regularly reconciled with the purchase ledger list of balances.

Task 2.11

A company wants to pay the right amount for goods purchased.	Control objective
A company reconciles supplier statements to the purchase ledger.	Control procedure
A company may pay for goods which are used for personal purposes.	Risk

Task 2.12

The company should pay employees for work done.	Control objective
The company could make incorrect payments to HMRC.	Risk
The company reviews payroll against budgets.	Control procedure

Task 2.13

The company buys assets it does not need.	Risk
Depreciation rates should reflect the useful life of an asset.	Control objective
The company keeps a non-current assets register.	Control procedure

Task 2.14

Goods inwards are checked and recorded.	Control procedure
Goods may be used for personal gain.	Risk
Goods are available when required for use in the business.	Control objective

Task 2.15

	✓
A graph	✓
A flowchart	
Narrative notes	
A questionnaire	

Auditors may record systems by using:

* Narrative notes
* Flowcharts
* Internal control questionnaires

Task 2.16

A walkthrough test is a test designed to ensure that the system | operates | as the | auditors | have been told that it does. They select a transaction in a particular area (for example, a sale or a purchase) and trace it through the company's information system from the initial point (for example, the sales | order | or the purchase | requisition |).

Task 2.17

Internal control questionnaire – revenue and receivables system

Question	Yes/No	Comment
Are orders only accepted from low credit risks?	Yes	Sales staff check that customers have not exceeded limits.
Are despatches checked by appropriate personnel?	Yes	Ian Jones checks order prior to despatch.
Are goods sent out recorded?	Yes	Ian Jones raises a despatch note.
Are customers required to give evidence of receipt of goods?	Yes	They are requested to sign a copy of the despatch note.
Are invoices checked to despatch notes and invoices?	Yes	The order and despatch note are matched prior to invoicing.

Question	Yes/No	Comment
Are invoices prepared using authorised prices?	Yes	The sales department has completed authorised prices on the order. Jane does not appear to carry out additional checks on invoices.
Are invoices checked to ensure they add up correctly?	No	Jane does not appear to carry out additional checks on invoices.
Are sales receipts matched with invoices?	No	No. Receipts are simply posted to the ledger and cashbook.
Are statements sent out regularly?	Yes	Monthly.
Are overdue accounts reviewed regularly?	No	No review appears to take place, but irrecoverable debts are rare.
Are there safeguards over post received to ensure that cheques are not intercepted?	No	Post is opened elsewhere and transferred to the accounts department.
Are bankings made daily?	No	However, cheques are kept securely until they are banked.
Would it be appropriate to perform tests of control in this area?	Yes	There appears to be a good system of control over ordering, despatch, invoicing and recording. Substantive tests should also be carried out over receipts and irrecoverable debts where controls are weakest.

Task 2.18

	Reliance ✓	No reliance ✓
A company where there is an internal audit function which monitors controls on a systematic and regular basis.	✓	
A small company where the owner-manager has virtual control over all accounting transactions, aided by his part-time, unqualified wife.		✓

Task 2.19

Management communicate controls values to staff and ensure new staff are thoroughly training in controls procedures.	Strong
Management emphasise the importance of targets over procedures.	Weak
Management include adherence to company procedures in annual appraisals for staff members.	Strong

Task 2.20

	Strength ✓	Deficiency ✓
Julie raises the sales invoices on the basis of the goods received notes she is sent by the warehouse. She inputs the information, prints the invoices, and sends them out. No other procedures are carried out.		✓ – She does not check the invoices prior to sending to check they are correct.
Statements are sent to customers on a monthly basis.	✓	

Task 2.21

Sandra reconciles supplier statements with the purchase ledger as she receives them.	Strength
Payments, which are approved by a director, are made on a monthly basis on the basis of a printout of due items from the purchase ledger.	Strength

Task 2.22

Each member of staff is allocated a personnel file on arrival, which is updated for any changes in pay rates or hours.	Strength
The payroll is created by the wages clerk on the last Thursday of a month. She runs the payroll package which automatically produces a bank payments list and notifies the bank to pay the salaries.	Deficiency – The payroll does not appear to be authorised by a senior member of staff.

Task 2.23

	Strength ✓	Deficiency ✓
The company maintains a non-current asset register. The operations manager checks the register to physical assets once a year.	✓	
The operations manager and the purchasing director meet monthly to discuss asset requirements for the business.	✓	

Task 2.24

Inventory is kept in a locked store, secured by the key card system in operation at the company. All members of staff are issued with key cards.	Deficiency – The inventory is available to any staff member unnecessarily. Access should be restricted.
The production manager reviews levels of inventory and makes requisitions on a monthly basis.	Deficiency – Critical inventory could run out during a month and cause business interruption. The company should have reorder levels which automatically trigger requisition.

Task 2.25

Internal control procedure	Risk mitigated
Credit checks are run on new customers.	Customers are not good credit risks.
Despatches are checked for quality before leaving the warehouse.	Customers are issued credit notes incorrectly.

Task 2.26

Risk	Internal control procedure to mitigate
Company pays for poor quality goods	Company reviews all goods inwards for condition
Company pays for the same invoice twice	Company records payments promptly on the purchases ledger

Chapter 3

Task 3.1

An auditor needs to obtain sufficient, appropriate evidence.	True
Sufficient means evidence from at least two sources.	False

Task 3.2

	Test of control ✓	Substantive procedure ✓
Observation of inventory count	✓	
Inspection of invoices to vouch cost of new non-current assets		✓
Recalculation of depreciation charge		✓

Task 3.3

	Test of control ✓	Substantive procedure ✓
A test to verify the operation of procedures designed to safeguard the business.	✓	
A comparison of financial and non-financial information by the auditor.		✓ (Analytical procedure)
A test to verify an assertion made in the financial statements.		✓

Task 3.4

Tests of controls

Controls	Tests of control
The company has a policy for choosing suppliers.	Review a sample of orders. – To ensure that the suppliers appear on the approved list.
Goods received are examined for quantity and quality.	Observe the store manager receiving some goods. – To ensure that they are examined properly.
Goods received are checked against the order.	Observe the store manager receiving some goods. – To ensure he checks the order. Review a sample of orders. – To see if he has noted the check (by initialling for example).

Task 3.5

Tests of controls

Controls	Tests of control
Hours worked are recorded.	Review clockcards – They are evidence of hours being recorded.
Hours worked are reviewed.	Review clockcards – To look for evidence of authorisation.
Payroll is prepared by a director.	Review payroll – To check that it is indeed prepared by the director.

Task 3.6

Non-current assets	Analytical procedures
Inventory	Tests of details
Receivables	Tests of details
Bank	Analytical procedures
Payables	Tests of details

The following items will require testing because they are above the materiality limit (£70,000):

- Inventory
- Receivables
- Payables falling due in less than one year

However, non-current assets and cash should also be reviewed in case they contain an error of understatement which is material.

....

Task 3.7

Non-current assets	Tests of details
Inventory	Tests of details
Receivables	Analytical procedures
Bank	Tests of details
Trade payables	Tests of details
Accruals	Analytical procedures
Bank loan	Tests of details

The following balances are material and should be tested in detail:

- Non-current assets
- Inventory
- Trade payables
- Bank loan

In addition, the bank balance has gone into overdraft which is a major difference from last year. This balance should also be tested in detail, although it is immaterial.

The receivables balance and the accruals balances are immaterial and have not changed significantly from the previous year, therefore it should only be tested by analytical procedures.

Task 3.8

Description on the invoice.	Classification
Date on the invoice.	Cut off

Task 3.9

Selection of a sample of sales ledger accounts over £30,000	Audit software
Input of sales invoices with false customer numbers to ensure application controls function correctly	Test data
Analytical procedures on statement of profit or loss, on a line by line approach	Audit software

Task 3.10

When sampling, the auditor must ensure that all sampling items have an equal chance of selection.	True
When an auditor selects a sample of invoices at random from the filed invoices for the year, this is known as the random approach to sampling.	False – This is haphazard selection.

Task 3.11

	Effect on sample size
The auditor intends to increase his reliance on tests of controls.	Increase
The auditor is selecting a sample of sales invoices, when a new customer means the volume of sales at the client has increased by 20%.	No effect
The auditors' tolerable deviation rate rises from 1.5% to 2%.	Decrease

Task 3.12

Obtain evidence of the completeness of the trade payables balance	Purchase requisition
Obtain evidence that the bank balance is fairly stated	Bank letter

Task 3.13

	True ✓	False ✓
The auditor may take a combined approach, where he will test controls and then reduce his subsequent substantive testing (although he must always carry out tests of detail on material items).	✓	
The auditor may take a substantive approach, where he does not test controls, but instead renders control risk as high and conducts more tests of detail instead.	✓	

Task 3.14

	Reliance ✓	No reliance ✓
The directors of LightLynx Ltd demand close attention to control procedures, and they monitor how the system is operating on a monthly basis.	✓	
At Simlaglow Ltd, there is an accounting staff of two, the financial controller, and his assistant.		✓ – There are insufficient staff for adequate segregation of duties.
There are ten people in the accounts department at Luxicon Ltd. The financial controller keeps a close interest in all transactions, and often intervenes to speed up proceedings.		✓ – There is a suggestion of management override of controls here.

Task 3.15

Financial statement assertion	Example test
Completeness	(a) Review of events after the end of the reporting period (b) Cut off testing for events (c) Analytical procedures for inventory (d) Confirmations (e) Reconciliations to control account (f) Sequence checks (g) Review of reciprocal populations
Rights and obligations	(a) Checking invoices for proof that item belongs to the company (b) Confirmations with third parties
Cut-off	(a) Match up last GRNs with purchase invoices to ensure liability is recorded in the correct period (b) Match up last GDNs with sales invoices to ensure income is recorded in the correct period

Financial statement assertion	Example test
Existence	(a) Physical verification (b) Third party confirmations (c) Cut off testing
Occurrence	(a) Inspection of supporting documentation (b) Confirmation from directors that transactions relate to business (c) Inspection of items purchased
Accuracy, valuation and allocation	(a) Re-calculation of correct amounts for both transactions and assets (eg checking invoices for correct purchase price) (b) Third party confirmation (c) Expert valuation (d) Analytical procedures (e) Confirming that accounting policies are consistent and reasonable (f) Review of post period end payments and invoices (g) Review cash received for correct allocation to appropriate trade receivable accounts
Classification	(a) Check compliance with Companies Act and accounting standards (b) Review classification of inventory between raw materials, work in progress and finished goods to ensure consistency with underlying financial records
Presentation	(a) Review disclosures for going concern to ensure consistency with audit procedures (b) Review disclosures for cash to ensure any legal rights of set-off have been correctly shown

Chapter 4

Task 4.1

Auditors are required to obtain an understanding of the entity and its environment only when the client is a new client.	False
Auditors are required to obtain an understanding of the entity and its environment so that they are able to assess the risks relating to the audit.	True

Task 4.2

Audit risk is the risk that the auditors give an inappropriate opinion on the financial statements. It is made up of three components:

- Inherent risk – risks arising as a result of the nature of the business, its transactions and environment

- Control risk – the risk that the control system at the company does not detect, correct or prevent misstatements

 (These two risks combined are the risk that misstatements will exist in the financial statements in the first place.)

- Detection risk – the risk that auditors do not discover misstatements in the financial statements

Task 4.3

	✓
Identify inherent and control risks while obtaining an understanding of the entity	
Relate identified risks to what could go wrong at a financial statement level	
Consider if the risks could cause material misstatement	
Identify detection risk as part of a review of audit firm procedure	✓

Detection risk is not so much identified as calculated based on the risk of material misstatement identified at the client. It is specific to the particular audit.

The auditor will take the following steps:

(1) Identify inherent and control risks while obtaining an understanding of the entity

(2) Relate identified risks to what could go wrong at a financial statement level

(3) Consider if the risks are so big they could cause material misstatement

Task 4.4

At a financial statement level:

- Items can be understated or overstated.
- Items requiring disclosure can be omitted.

Task 4.5

Sales revenue has increased by 3% but the gross profit margin is down by 1.5%.	More information required to draw a conclusion
Sales in the last month of the year were 5% higher than in previous years, and also 4% higher than the average for a month for the company.	Sales revenue may be overstated

Task 4.6

Shop 1 sales income is £2,521,634.	Appear reasonable
Cafe sales income is £431,996.	Appear reasonable
Total sales income is £5,673,676.	Understated

Workings

Shop 1 sales income estimate:

April (30) + May (31) + June (30) + July (31) = 122 days × 400 × £30 = £1,464,000

February (28 assuming this is not a leap year) + March (31) + August (31) + September (30) = 120 days × 300 × £20 = £720,000

October (31) + November (30) + December (31) + January (31) = 123 days × 200 × £15 = £369,000

Total Shop 1 for 12 months = £1,464,000 + £720,000 + £369,000 = **£2,553,000**

The recorded sales amount of £2,521,634 only varies from this estimate by 1.2% so the recorded amount appears reasonable by comparison.

Café sales income estimate:

(122 days × 400) = 48,800
(120 days × 300) = 36,000
(123 days × 200) = 24,600
48,800 + 36,000 + 24,600 = 109,400/2 = 54,700 × £8 = **£437,600**

The recorded sales amount of £431,996 only varies from this estimate by 1.3% so the recorded amount appears reasonable by comparison.

Shop 2 sales income estimate:

£2,553,000 × 75% = **£1,914,750**

Shop 3 sales income estimate:

£2,553,000 × 65% = **£1,659,450**

Total sales income estimate = **£2,553,000 + £437,600 + £1,914,750 + £1,659,450 = £6,564,800**

The recorded sales amount of £5,673,676 varies from this estimate by 13.6% so the recorded amount appears understated by comparison.

Task 4.7

The company issues inventory to customers on a sale or return basis.	Assets could be over- or understated – The company might forget to include inventory which is at the third party, or might include inventory that the third party has actually sold.
The non-current asset register is not reconciled regularly with the actual assets.	Assets could be over- or understated – Assets might be missing or obsolete, or assets might have been bought and not included in the register.

Task 4.8

	Increase ✓	Reduce ✓
The company operates in a highly regulated industry.	✓	
The company has an internal audit function committed to monitoring internal controls.		✓
The company has set ambitious growth targets for all its salesmen, to be judged at the end of the financial year.	✓	

Task 4.9

	Increase ✓	Decrease ✓
The role of sales ledger clerk has been filled by four different people during the year, following the retirement of a long-standing sales ledger clerk at the end of last year.	✓	
The financial controller is a qualified accountant, as are two of his high level staff.		✓
The directors have a positive attitude towards controls and enforce them company-wide.		✓

Task 4.10

A control such as a [password] may [prevent] unauthorised access to a computer programme so that errors cannot be deliberately input.

Alternatively a control such as a reconciliation [detects] mistakes, which the person carrying out the reconciliation can then [correct], so that there is no misstatement in the financial statements as a result.

Task 4.11

	True ✓	False ✓
Materiality is the concept of importance to users.	✓	
It is relevant to auditors because they will only test items which are material.		✓ – Materiality contributes to sample selection but some immaterial items will be tested to ensure that overall the financial statements are materially fairly stated.
Calculating materiality and selecting samples on the basis of materiality helps the auditor to reduce audit risk to an acceptable level.	✓ – This is the relationship between materiality and audit risk.	

Task 4.12

	✓
A risk of fraud	
A complex transaction	
A significant transaction with a related party	
A transaction in the normal course of business for the entity	✓

This does not suggest a significant risk – a significant risk might be indicated by a transaction outside the normal course of business for an entity.

Task 4.13

Material and pervasive is taken to mean that the misstatement is:

- [Not confined] to one item in the financial statements.

- [Confined] to one item, but the item could represent a substantial portion of the financial statements.

- If relating to a disclosure, [fundamental] to users' understanding of the financial statements.

Chapter 5

Task 5.1

This answer gives three risks to show the range of answers that you might have given:

Audit risk	Potential impact on financial statements
The company relies heavily on two customers. One of the customers is currently reviewing Glad Rags to ensure it meets the required qualities of being a quality supplier.	Going concern issues if the company were to lose this custom
The company relies heavily on the involvement of the sole director, Gladys, who is considering selling the company.	Dominance of an individual director can reduce effectiveness of internal control systems, which could cause error throughout the financial statements.

Gladys' plans to sell the company could have implications for going concern, if she does not find a buyer for the company.

Gladys' plans to sell the company could lead to a desire to bias the financial statements so that the company looks like a good investment. |
| The control system is restricted by the low number of administrative staff involved and there appears to be limited segregation of duties in the accounts department. | Lack of segregation of duties can result in errors not being detected by the control systems and therefore arising anywhere in the financial statements. This would cast concern particularly on sales revenue/receivables and purchases/payables, which are all likely to be material balances. |

Task 5.2

	✓
Obtain a summary of non-current assets and reconcile with the opening position (additions and disposals)	
Compare non-current assets in the general ledger with the non-current asset register and obtain explanations for any differences	
Inspect assets to see if they are in use and good condition	✓
Check that assets which physically exist are included in the register	

Inspect assets to see if they are in use and good condition – this is a test for either existence or accuracy, valuation and allocation.

Task 5.3

Review depreciation rates for reasonableness (given asset lives, residual values, replacement policy, possible obsolescence)	Accuracy, valuation and allocation
Vouch title deeds of buildings	Rights and obligations
Inspect a sample of assets listed in the non-current assets register	Existence

Task 5.4

Client: Kandistors Limited	Prepared by:
Year-end: 31 December 20X3	Reviewed by:
Subject: Non-current assets	Date:

Objective	Test	Completed by
Completeness	(1) Ensure **opening balances** in **accounting records agree to last year's accounts**	
	(2) **Check** that the **assets seen** at the client's **premises** have been **recorded** in **the non-current asset register**	
	(3) **Compare** the **non-current asset register** with the **non-current asset accounts** in the ledger, and check that **differences** in **value** can be **satisfactorily explained**	
	(4) **Review repairs, maintenance** and **sundry expenditure** during the year, and **enquire** into **any expenditure** that looks as if it should have been **capitalised**	
	(5) Compare actual **non-current asset expenditure** with **budgeted expenditure** and **obtain explanations** for differences	
	(6) **Check** that all **non-current asset expenditure** shown as authorised in the board minutes has been made	
Existence	(1) **Inspect a sample of assets** that are **recorded** in the non-current **asset register**	
	(2) **Examine invoices** for **smaller furniture and equipment additions** to see if any have been **incorrectly capitalised**	

Objective	Test	Completed by
Rights and obligations	(1) **Inspect title deeds** for land and buildings	
	(2) **Inspect other documentation** (vehicle registration documents, insurance policies) for evidence of title to other assets	
	(3) Inspect **purchase invoices**, records of **assets received** and **solicitors' completion statements** for **assets purchased** during the year to see if they are in the client's name and purchases have been properly authorised	
	(4) **Review bank letter** for details of assets and title documents held	
Accuracy, valuation and allocation	(1) When inspecting assets, note any **signs of undue wear** or **lack of use**	
	(2) **Examine purchase invoices** for evidence of costs of assets purchased during the year	

Note. Based on the information available at the time this book was written, we anticipate a task like this would be human marked in the real assessment.

Task 5.5

Tests to be carried out on non-current assets at Craftys:

Completeness

- Compare non-current assets in the general ledger with the non-current asset register and reconcile any differences

- Select a sample of assets which physically exist and trace them to the non-current asset register

- Review sensitive balances in the statement of profit or loss (such as repairs or motor costs) to ensure items which should have been capitalised have not been expensed in the year

Rights and obligations

- Review title deeds for land and buildings
- Check a sample of registration documents for company vehicles

Existence

- Select a sample of assets from the non-current asset register and trace the physical assets
- Inspect the assets to ensure they exist, and are in good condition and use

Accuracy, valuation and allocation

As assets have not been revalued, focus testing on additions:

- Check the purchase invoices for the new vehicles and fittings
- Review depreciation rates to ensure they are reasonable
- Recalculate depreciation to ensure it has been correctly calculated
- Ensure value of major land and buildings assets has not been impaired

Note. Based on the information available at the time this book was written, we anticipate a task like this would be human marked in the real assessment.

Task 5.6

	✓
£69,000	
£57,000	
£33,000	✓
£25,000	

The replacement engine and the new software both sound like capital items.

Task 5.7

	✓
The inventory count	✓
Inventory records	
The locked stores	
The reorder levels	

Task 5.8

The company records a sale but the inventory is also counted as existing at the year end.	(a) Profit is overstated (b) Assets are overstated
The company accept goods on the day of the inventory count, which get included in the count, but do not record the invoice in purchases until the following year.	(a) Profit is overstated (b) Liabilities are understated

Task 5.9

The auditors will need to verify:

- The initial cost of the raw materials (usually tested by reference to original purchase invoices)

- The cost of conversion to finished goods (for example, labour costs, usually tested by reference to time records and the payroll, and overhead costs, usually tested by reference to overall overhead costs and the invoices for these costs)

Task 5.10

	✓
Ensuring inventory which appeared damaged at the inventory count has been valued accordingly	
Examine sales prices after the year end to ensure that none have significantly dropped (perhaps to below cost)	
Review quantities of inventory sold after the year end to ensure that goods are not obsolete	
Review sales prices during the year to ensure that none have been significantly low	✓

It is the value of items at the year end that the auditors are concerned with.

Task 5.11

(a) **Inventory count – key issues**

The count instructions must be reviewed and the count should be observed to ensure that the instructions are followed.

A sample of the counts should be test-checked that the checkers have made. Last year's sample was 12. As Joe Worple has stated that there are no major changes in inventory this year, the same sample size should be used.

Attention should be focused on raw materials, which is likely to be a higher amount in total than finished goods. In particular, the specialist fabric A001 should be included within the test count, as well as the major inventory lines of S01, CJ02 and CJ03. Given that the store manager has said there are no major changes in inventory, these items should be high value as they were last year.

Some finished goods should be selected within the sample as the overall value of finished goods may be higher than raw materials, although the quantity is smaller and ensure that, as instructed, no work in progress exists.

Some items should be remeasured during the count to ensure that the controls over the amount of fabric operate effectively, for example based on an initial sample of five bales. A sample of the records on the bales should also be reviewed to ensure that they are arithmetically accurate.

The main count will be taking place in the stores, so the auditor should meet Mr Worple there. However, the auditor should also attend the machine room at 3pm to ensure that all operations have finished before the count starts.

Lastly, details of the last delivery from the factory and the last delivery to the factory before the count should be obtained to enable inventory cut off tests to be carried out at the final audit.

(b) **Review of count instructions**

The instructions show that the count has been well thought out and appears organised. There are good controls over checks and to ensure that items are not counted twice. Controls to prevent movements of inventory during the count appear to be sound. Provided the count is carried out according to the instructions, the count should be capable of providing a suitable figure for inventory existence.

The key control is the existing control over quantity of inventory, which is that the bales are marked down for fabric removed and most of it is not remeasured at the count. The auditors must be satisfied that this control is operating effectively to be able to rely on the count.

Therefore, it is important to check both that the record attached to the inventory tallies with the amount of inventory present and that the records are arithmetically accurate.

Note. Based on the information available at the time this book was written, we anticipate a task like this would be human marked in the real assessment.

Task 5.12

Identify the appropriate conclusion to draw about inventory cut off at this stage by selecting the appropriate option.	Cut off is fairly stated

An error was discovered in purchase cut off. One invoice, value £2,476, was included in December purchases in error. This is not material, but should be included on a schedule of non-material potential adjustments.

Task 5.13

Identify which of the tests needs to be carried out to draw a conclusion as to whether the existence of inventory is fairly stated by selecting the appropriate option.	Trace test count items to final inventory sheets

Task 5.14

(a)   Risks

- Damaged raw materials may be valued too high.

- Raw materials may be valued inappropriately.

- The level and percentage completion of WIP at count date may be miscalculated.

- Inventory for customer in financial difficulties may be obsolete (unless it is suitably non-specific to be sold to other parties).

(b) **Procedures relating to inventory valuation**

At inventory count:

- Identify and record damaged inventory and potentially obsolete inventory

- Identify WIP and assess degree of completion

At final audit:

- Ensure items noted at inventory count included in final inventory sheets

- Ensure obsolete items assigned no or suitably reduced value

- Verify costs of sample of raw materials to appropriate invoices for accounting method

- Consider whether accounting method for cost appropriate for raw materials

- Verify costs of WIP to payroll and overhead documentation such as purchase invoices

- Assess whether appropriate percentage completeness has been calculated for cost

- Review business after the year end with troubled customer (check sales orders/invoices/receipts) to see if inventory was sold/paid for and should be valued in financial statements

- Perform general NRV review of sales in next year

Note. Based on the information available at the time this book was written, we anticipate a task like this would be human marked in the real assessment.

Task 5.15

	✓
X13639443 only	
FG135933 and X1369443 only	✓
R0204863 and FG135934 only	
FG135934 only	

Task 5.16

Audit procedures

Existence – controls:

- Attend a scheduled count (any of the four in the year).
- Ensure count instructions suggest controls over count are good.
- Ensure count instructions are followed.
- Ensure only goods that should be counted are counted.
- Ensure that inventory movements are minimised during the count.

Existence – substantive:

- Attend the company on 31 December and test count a sample of inventory items from inventory records to actual inventory and vice versa.

- Ensure that a list of inventory on hand on 31 December is retained for the purposes of the final audit.

Completeness:

- Select a sample of goods in before and after year end (per inventory records) and trace them to the purchase ledger to ensure that the purchases are recorded in the same period as the goods in.

- Select a sample of goods out before and after the year end (per inventory records) and trace them to the sales ledger to ensure that sales are recorded in the same period as goods out.

Note. Based on the information available at the time this book was written, we anticipate a task like this would be human marked in the real assessment.

Task 5.17

	✓
(i) only	
(i) and (ii) only	
(i), (ii), (iii) and (iv) only	
All of them	✓

Task 5.18

Audit of the valuation of receivables

Valuation of receivables can be tested by scrutinising the cash paid subsequent to the year end. Auditors will be particularly concerned with older receivables on the ledger, especially when subsequent receivables have been paid, as this may indicate that the old receivable is not likely to be paid and has therefore been overvalued.

Audit procedures:

(1) Obtain an aged receivable analysis from the sales ledger at 30 November.

(2) Scrutinise it to identify receivables greater than 60 days old at 30 November (60 days being the standard payment period of Glad Rags' customers).

(3) Review the cash book for evidence of the old receivables being paid.

(4) If some old receivables are still unpaid as at the middle of January, they must be discussed with the accountant to assess whether action has been taken.

(5) Scrutinise any correspondence with the late payer.

(6) Consider any allowance made for irrecoverable debts and assess whether it is sufficient.

(7) Identify any further adjustments that might need to be made in respect of irrecoverable debts and write them on the schedule of unadjusted errors.

Note. Based on the information available at the time this book was written, we anticipate a task like this would be human marked in the real assessment.

Task 5.19

(a) Risks

(i) It is possible that at planning date Diversity Ltd is in arrears for its first payment owed to Carl Ltd, although depending on the exact timings of invoices, as Diversity only became a customer in the last quarter, it may not quite be.

(ii) Diversity is a new customer with no history with Carl, and there is a risk that despite the credit checks that were carried out (and as Diversity is a new company, these may not have been very detailed) that Diversity is a bad credit risk and its debt will be overstated in the financial statements.

(iii) This is backed up by speculation in the press that the company does not have the working capital to sustain operations.

(iv) In addition, Carl Ltd's staff have requested that we do not seek direct confirmation of Diversity's balance, which restricts our audit work, and could mean, particularly in the absence of a payment pattern that it is difficult to obtain audit evidence in this area.

(v) This could lead to there being a limitation in scope on our audit (as we are being prevented from obtaining evidence that would normally be available to us). However, if Diversity continue to be in arrears and we explain the seriousness to us of a lack of direct evidence, it is likely that the company will contact Diversity on our behalf (particularly since if the situation perpetuates itself, the credit controller will have to contact Diversity to request payment of the debt).

(b) Procedures

(i) Review sales ledger receipts subsequent to audit planning date to see if Diversity have paid the balance or established a payment pattern (for example, a significant proportion of the debt may have been paid by the time of the audit).

(ii) Discuss Diversity's failure to keep to their credit terms with Carl Ltd's credit controller to see if she has had discussions and/or correspondence with the customer.

(iii) Review correspondence if any.

(iv) Corroborate any matters referred to in correspondence (for example, credits requested/credit notes).

(v) Consider whether an allowance is required if receivable appears irrecoverable.

Note. Based on the information available at the time this book was written, we anticipate a task like this would be human marked in the real assessment.

- -

Task 5.20

(a) BCS difference | Bank statements |

(b) Tisco stores difference | Goods returned note |

- -

Task 5.21

Bank letter requests should be made by the ...	auditors.
Bank letter requests should be sent to the bank ...	a month before the year end.

Task 5.22

| Window dressing | is the practice of manipulating when cash receipts and payments are recorded and sent out to manipulate the | statement of financial position | results at the year end.

For example, if a company wanted liabilities to look | lower | then it might record a number of payments (which would also therefore be included on the bank reconciliation, reducing the bank balance) but not physically send those cheques out until after the year end, so that in practice, the bank balance is | higher | than it appears to be in the accounts, as is the | payables | balance.

Task 5.23

	✓
Pre year end cash book	
Post year end cash book	
Pre year end bank statements	
Post year end bank statements	✓

Task 5.24

	✓
Compare opening balances to the previous year's working papers (closing balances at the end of last year)	
Examine receipts for loan repayments	✓
Compare balances to the general ledger	
Review minutes and cashbook to ensure that all loans have been recorded	

Examining the receipts issued by lenders for the repayment of loan amounts is a test of accuracy, valuation and allocation.

Task 5.25

Current liabilities	£1,200
Non-current liabilities	£3,700

Workings

The 5-year loan agreement was signed on 1/2/X9 and no repayments were made until 1/8/X9 meaning the loan is repaid over 4½ years at a rate of £100 per month. The total amount borrowed is therefore (4½ years × 12 months × £100) = £5,400.

As at 31/12/X9, Anderson has repaid £500 meaning the **total liability** is £4,900 split between **current liabilities** (those falling due in the next 12 months) of £1,200 and the balance of **non-current liabilities** of £3,700 (£4,900 – £1,200).

Task 5.26

Supplier statements provide excellent third party evidence about trade payables.	True
Suppliers are circularised in the same way as receivables.	False – In fact this is rare, because supplier statements provide excellent evidence.

Task 5.27

	✓
When internal controls over purchases are weak and the auditor suspects that the trade payables balance has been understated.	✓
When internal controls over purchases are strong and the auditor suspects that the trade payables balance has been understated.	
When internal controls over purchases are weak and the auditor suspects that the trade payables balance has been overstated.	
When internal controls over purchases are strong and the auditor suspects that the trade payables balance has been overstated.	

Task 5.28

Audit objective	Audit test
Test completeness of purchases	Trace sample of purchases from initial records to financial statements
Test understatement of payables	Reconcile purchase ledger with supplier statements

Task 5.29

Payment not on supplier statement	Both bank statement and cash book – The cash book will give evidence that the payment was made through the books prior to the year end. The auditor will also wish to ensure that the payment cleared early in May (ie that the timing of the payment is genuine).
Invoice 1812	Purchase invoice – This should have the GRN attached to it as controls are good. The date of goods receipt determines whether there is a liability at year end date.

Task 5.30

Payables testing at Johnny's Juices Ltd

- Obtain payables ledger listing and check for arithmetical accuracy

- Perform analytical procedures on payables balance (compare with prior years)

- If there are unexpected fluctuations, request monthly purchases information and ensure it ties in with sales patterns

- If analytical procedures do not provide satisfactory evidence concerning payables balance, it may be necessary to reconstruct year end balance by reviewing invoices and payment records

Note. Based on the information available at the time this book was written, we anticipate a task like this would be human marked in the real assessment.

Task 5.31

	True ✓	False ✓
Auditors often perform analytical procedures when auditing sales revenue as there is usually a great deal of analytical information about sales revenue (for example, analyses of sales per month or per product) at a company, and sales revenue has a number of predictable relationships (with receivables, with gross margin) so it is a good balance to test by analytical procedures.	✓	
Auditors may test understatement of sales revenue by tracing a sale from the general ledger back through the system to the sales order.		✓ – Understatement is tested by starting with source documents (for example, sales orders).

Task 5.32

(a) **Risk**: Suppliers might be slow in submitting their invoices and therefore it may be difficult to ensure that all liabilities at the year end are recorded in the correct period.

(b) **Objectives**: The key audit objective is to ensure that all relevant liabilities are recorded in the correct period.

(c) **Procedures**: A standard purchase cut-off procedure would be to take a sample of goods received notes for an appropriate period before the year end and after the year end and trace these to suppliers' invoices and payables records and the purchase ledger to confirm that the relevant liabilities are taken up in the correct year.

Note. Based on the information available at the time this book was written, we anticipate a task like this would be human marked in the real assessment.

Task 5.33

	✓
Recalculate the accruals	
Verify accruals by reference to previous payments	✓
Verify accruals by reference to subsequent payments	
Compare accruals in current statement of profit or loss and prior years	

Task 5.34

	✓
£0	
£6,000	✓
£15,000	
£60,000	

Task 5.35

(a) Warranty provision

- Obtain draft financial statements and compare current provision to previous year

- Compare current sales volumes with previous year to establish likely demand for warranty

- Investigate number of products where warranties have been claimed by customers

- Establish costs associated with repairs and compare with warranty provision

- Discuss method of calculating warranty provision with management to establish rationale behind amounts posted in financial statements

(b) Payroll overpayments

- Obtain summary of current payroll costs by name and vouch a sample of staff paid to personnel records

- Discuss process for removing leavers from payroll with relevant staff to ensure the system is robust

- Enquire about existence of procedures for monitoring payroll costs (such as budgetary control) in order to identify possible overpayments

(c) Prepaid telephone line rental

- Obtain summary of prepaid line rental amounts and compare to previous periods for consistency

- Verify amounts paid to most recent invoices and bank statement

- Recalculate the prepaid amount to ensure it reflects the period of line rental in the next year

- Review statement of profit or loss to ensure it only includes amounts for the current year

Note. Based on the information available at the time this book was written, we anticipate a task like this would be human marked in the real assessment.

Task 5.36

SILK Ltd is a new client which means there are the following risks:

- Lack of knowledge and understanding of the business

- Increased detection risk

- Failure to identify events and transactions which impact on the financial statements/spot errors

- Opening balances may be misstated

The company pays for ingredients in overseas currency, which means there is a risk of inappropriate exchange rates/translation errors in purchases, payables and inventory. The company also makes sales across the world which represents a risk of misstated sales revenues for the same reasons.

The acquisition of the newly acquired company presents risks of misstatement depending on the method of funding; equity may be misstated if new shares have been issued, while long-term liabilities might be misstated if the acquisition was debt-funded.

The consolidation may be complex and lead to misstatement across many account balances, such as goodwill, post-acquisition reserves, fair value adjustments and intra-group balances. The process of consolidation may also create misstatement if the method of consolidation is not appropriate (depending on the number of shares acquired and hence the amount of control and ownership that should be used).

The rationalisation process after the acquisition may leave staff or equipment surplus to requirements in manufacturing sites that are no longer deemed viable, leading to impairments in non-current assets and possible liabilities for staff redundancies.

Research and development presents a risk of misstatement due to the need to satisfy the requirements of IAS 38 *Intangible Assets* – given the newly acquired company also has a series of well-known brands, some existing products may no longer be developed and this may lead to misstatements in the statement of financial position if development does not proceed and capitalised expenditure needs to be written off.

Brands are also an area where misstatements might occur within intangible assets. There may be some new brands whose values would need to be assessed by an expert if they have now been acquired by SILK Ltd and require recognition on the statement of financial position.

Competition regulations may exist which forbid any one company from exerting monopolistic behaviour in a jurisdiction, so revenues and costs may be affected if SILK Ltd can no longer operate in a location where the new group is felt to be dominant.

Task 5.37

The company pays for holidays (travel costs, catering and accommodation) in overseas currency which means there is a risk of inappropriate exchange rates/translation errors in purchases and payables.

Deposits are taken by Golden Ltd for holidays that have not yet happened, which could lead to the risk of overstated revenue if such deferred income is recognised too soon. The situation regarding customers who are demanding the return of their deposits could also lead to the risk of overstated revenue in the statement of profit or loss if the company does not accurately reflect the extent of any deposits due to be returned.

The plane crash presents a number of audit risks:

(a) The value of aircraft in non-current assets may be overstated if it includes any material balances where aircraft have been either damaged or judged to be impaired due to any faults identified as a result of the crash.

(b) There may be additional costs to make good any damage/faults in the aircraft that could lead to understated costs/overstated profits.

(c) There may be overstated revenue if the company recognises revenue without fulfilling all its holiday commitments.

(d) There may be costs from affected passengers (lawsuits and associated expenses) which the company may need to make a provision for which could be understated.

(e) The removal of the company's licence to fly may affect its ability to continue operating (see below) or, at the very least, lead to fines and penalties that may not be included in costs and lead to understated expenses/overstated profits.

The cruise ship incident may also lead to legal action from those affected, both for damages and additional expenses incurred while in quarantine, which may lead to understated provisions and expenses (plus the risk of misstatement if contingent liabilities are not adequately disclosed in relation to these events).

However, of greatest concern to the auditors of Golden Ltd is the going concern status of the company as the combined effects of these incidents may mean that the company is unable to continue to trade for the foreseeable future and the financial statements may need to be prepared using an alternative basis (such as break up or liquidation).

Chapter 6

Task 6.1

Working papers are prepared by the external auditor because there is a professional requirement to do so.	True
The primary reason for recording work in working papers is so that senior staff members can review junior staff members' work.	False – This is a subsidiary benefit.
Working papers should record contentious issues and how they were resolved.	True

Task 6.2

Written representations are the written evidence of everything the directors have said to auditors during the audit.	False – It is written copy of certain required representations.
Auditors are required to get written confirmation from the directors of their responsibilities with regard to the financial statements.	True

Task 6.3

Working papers

Working papers are the documents on which auditors record their audit work. They may be paper format or on a computer.

Working papers must contain certain details. For example, they must state the name of the client, the year end being worked on, the name of the auditor doing the work and the date the work was done. They should also state the audit area, and contain the work done, the evidence obtained and conclusions drawn.

Task 6.4

	✓
No action as such 'consultancy' is normal business practice in that country	
Report the matter to the board of directors of Multicorp	
Report the matter to the audit engagement partner	
Report the matter to the firm's Money Laundering Reporting Officer	✓

This is a money laundering offence in the UK, despite where the bribery of government officials took place.

Task 6.5

In respect of this matter, select whether the audit junior should take no further action or refer to the supervisor.	Refer to supervisor – This could be indication of a fraud being carried out by the sales ledger clerk.

Task 6.6

In respect of this matter, select whether the audit junior should take no further action or refer to the supervisor.	No further action

Task 6.7

In respect of this matter, select whether the audit junior should take no further action or refer to the supervisor.	Refer to supervisor – The company may have been attempting to manipulate the statement of financial position.

Task 6.8

<table>
<tr>
<td>In respect of this matter, select whether the audit junior should take no further action or should refer to the supervisor.</td>
<td>Refer to supervisor
– The supplier may be fake suggesting a fraud being carried out in the purchase ledger.</td>
</tr>
</table>

Task 6.9

The identification of a fraud, relating to a material monetary amount, carried out by a director of the audited entity, which was not prevented by the entity's internal control system.

Significant deficiency

Task 6.10

The basic elements of the auditor's report

- A title, identifying to whom the audit report is addressed
- Addressee (normally the shareholders)
- Opinion and basis for opinion, plus a description of the scope of the audit
- Going concern, Key Audit Matters and other information
- A statement of management's responsibility for the financial statements
- A statement of the auditor's responsibility
- Legislative and regulatory matters
- Auditor's address and signature of the auditors
- Date of the signature

Task 6.11

The four possible types of opinion where there are matters that affect the auditor's opinion are:

(a) Qualified opinion: inability to obtain sufficient appropriate audit evidence (except for)

This qualified opinion is given where there has been an inability to obtain sufficient appropriate audit evidence in the auditors' work in one area. It is not considered to be pervasive but the auditor cannot give an opinion on it.

(b) Disclaimer of opinion

This opinion is given where the limitations on the scope of the auditors' work are so great that they cannot give an opinion on the truth and fairness of the financial statements.

(c) Qualified opinion: financial statements are materially misstated (except for)

This qualified opinion is given where misstatements have been identified in the financial statements, which are considered material but not pervasive.

(d) Adverse opinion

This opinion is given where the misstatements in the financial statements are so pervasive that the financial statements do not give a true and fair view.

Task 6.12

Identify whether the errors must be adjusted in order to issue an unmodified audit opinion on the financial statements by selecting the appropriate option.	Do not need to be adjusted – The first error should not be projected against the total as they do not affect the total balance. The other two are less than 5% of profit before tax, both individually and in aggregate.

Task 6.13

The directors refuse to write off a debt owed by Sandicore Ltd, a company that has gone into liquidation.	Qualified – This is restricted to receivables.
The auditors believe that the company is experiencing going concern issues. The directors have failed to disclose in the financial statements, claiming their recovery plan is going to get the company back on track. The auditors have reviewed cash flow forecasts covering a period of 12 months after the end of the accounting period and believe the assumptions made were reasonable. The auditors agree that the recovery plan has a high chance of success.	Qualified – The going concern disclosures have been omitted, rendering the financial statements misleading to users. However, the auditors do believe that it is correct for the financial statements to be prepared on a going concern basis, so an adverse opinion is unlikely to be required.

Task 6.14

Identify whether the financial statements appear to make sense.	Make sense

Task 6.15

Going concern

(1)   BCS:

- Enquire whether the audit has been completed and what the results were.

- Review any correspondence between BCS and Glad Rags.

- If BCS require Glad Rags to undertake certain matters, discuss with Gladys and consider whether Glad Rags is able to make the changes.

- Review the sales order book for the forthcoming period to assess whether BCS has withdrawn trade.

(2)   Potential sale of business:

- Discuss with Gladys her plans, in particular the timescale of those plans.

- Enquire if she intends to sell the business as a going concern and the likelihood of her being able to. Review any correspondence she has had with solicitors and or valuers/estate agents.

- Review budgets for the forthcoming year for Glad Rags Limited to ensure that the company appears to still be operating as a going concern.

- Discuss with Gladys whether she has implemented succession plans within the business, given that she is a key member of staff and integral to the business.

Note. Based on the information available at the time this book was written, we anticipate a task like this would be human marked in the real assessment.

Task 6.16

The auditors did not observe Handyco's inventory count at the year end, as they were not appointed until after that date. Due to the nature of the company's records, they have not been able to ascertain the existence of inventory by another method.	Modified – Inability to obtain sufficient appropriate audit evidence.
The auditors did not observe Complicateco's inventory count due to staffing difficulties on the day. The company has detailed inventory records, and the auditors were able to attend the premises two days later and carry out test counts against the company's records. The company had maintained a record of inventory existing on the year end date and movements since are easy to trace through the system.	Not modified – Alternative procedures are available.

Task 6.17

Deficiency: receipts

- Post opening appears to be unsupervised and no initial list of receipts is made.

- Customer remittances do not appear to be retained.

(a) Consequences

- Receipts could be lost or stolen on arrival at the company.

(b) Recommendations

- Ideally, someone from the accounts department should attend the opening of the post and make an initial list of receipts.

- Customer remittances should be retained so that receipts can be reconciled to specific invoices.

Note. Based on the information available at the time this book was written, we anticipate a task like this would be human marked in the real assessment.

Task 6.18

Present system

No passwords are required to access any part of the computerised accounting system.

(a) Consequences

Unrestricted access to the computer system could lead to error, deliberate alteration of accounting records, inefficiency and possible fraud.

(b) Recommendation

Your present software includes the facility to allow restricted access to systems by your staff through a structured system of passwords that can be changed frequently.

We recommend that passwords should be introduced as soon as possible.

Present system

Whilst security backup copies of files are taken, these copies are kept in the desk occupied by the accounts clerk.

(a) Consequences

Files may be lost, damaged or accessed without authorisation.

(b) Recommendation

We recommend that backup files are stored securely, for example, in a fire-proof safe.

Note. Based on the information available at the time this book was written, we anticipate a task like this would be human marked in the real assessment.

. . . .

Task 6.19

Central list of suppliers not used

(a) Consequences

Using non-approved suppliers might result in the following problems:

- Less favourable terms for the business (for example, credit terms, leading to cash flow problems)

- Lower quality goods being purchased leading to problems in production

- Less reliable delivery leading to problems in production

(b) Recommendations

(i) As there seems to be a team in the purchasing department at Miraglow, I would recommend that deals that seem to be good value to the company are referred to a nominated member of staff.

(ii) This individual can investigate whether all aspects of the deal are likely to benefit Miraglow and obtain references/check credentials of the company, and then notify the directors to get approval for using the new supplier, rather than using lots of different suppliers on an ad hoc basis.

Note. Based on the information available at the time this book was written, we anticipate a task like this would be human marked in the real assessment.

. . . .

Task 6.20

Possible consequences:

(a) Without adequate procedures for dealing with starters and leavers, there is a risk that staff may be paid incorrectly once they have started or that leavers may continue to be paid after they have left (new starters who are underpaid are most likely to complain, so overpayments are the biggest risk here).

(b) Staffing issues could lead to fraud and/or error in the processing of payroll information (this is exacerbated by the lack of segregation of duties presented by the same staff performing both HR and payroll activities without supervision and review).

(c) As above, fraud and/or error could occur due to this lack of internal control. In addition, failure to safeguard employee's confidential details could lead to sanctions if the company fails to comply with data protection legislation.

(d) The new computerised system may include processing errors that have not yet been spotted, which could lead to problems with record-keeping and potential overpayments, as well as errors in the transfer of data.

(e) It is possible that statutory deductions (such as tax and national insurance) have not been made correctly, leading to possible misstatement of relevant amounts in the financial statements and potential fines from the tax authorities.

Recommendations:

(a) A suitable independent resource (such as internal audit if they exist) should perform an analysis of starters and leavers (such as tracing the first and last payment made to each one) going back over recent months to determine whether any overpayments have occurred and then attempt to quantify any misstatements.

(b) A selection of payroll records should be reviewed for compliance with policy and procedure (if any exist) and the extent of any fraud and/or error quantified (in the short term, this should again be completed by internal audit to maintain independence). Moving forward, staffing levels in both HR and payroll should be reviewed as a priority

(c) As above, a review of record-keeping should be completed as a priority and the extent of any breaches in legislation should be established.

(d) A post-implementation review should be undertaken as a priority to establish whether there are any misstatements in the payroll and whether the system is operating as intended (staff may require training in the new system so human error should be considered as well).

(e) A reconciliation of deductions made compared to deductions due should be completed by internal audit to determine the extent of any misstatement and necessary training of payroll staff should be arranged as soon as possible.

Task 6.21

Possible consequences:

(a) The absence of onsite management could lead to poor practices being adopted by staff at Jump.

(b) Without employing parking wardens, Jump could be missing out on revenue due from parking.

(c) Cash collection appears to lack segregation of duties and could be subject to either fraud or error due to inadequate numbers of staff performing this activity (the amounts of cash handled by Jump could be significant too, making this a significant risk).

(d) Maintenance of the gym equipment and swimming pool is not carried out by qualified staff, leading to the risk of negligence if the public use faulty equipment and are injured as a result.

(e) It is possible that Jump's pool is using more water than it should and that levels of chemicals used in the water may be inappropriate for general use and may not comply with health and safety regulations.

(f) The accident book process does not seem to differentiate between staff and users of the leisure facilities, and causes are not listed, meaning that any necessary action may not be properly identified.

Recommendations:

(a) The Head of Leisure Services should consider managing Jump from onsite.

(b) Wardens (or similar) should be costed up and employed if cost-effective.

(c) Cash collection staff should be costed up and employed if cost-effective.

(d) The adequacy of the current Fidelity Guarantee Insurance cover should be assessed by comparison to the amounts of cash handled regularly.

(e) Existing staff should be trained or specialist staff recruited to maintain all equipment at Jump.

(f) Specialist pool management knowledge should be provided to staff (see above) via training.

(g) More details should be recorded in the accident book ie staff/public; cause of accident; and need for remedial work at Jump etc.

AAT AQ2016 SAMPLE ASSESSMENT 1
EXTERNAL AUDITING

Time allowed: 2 hours

External Auditing: AAT sample assessment 1

Task 1 (2 marks)

Identify the level of assurance provided by the following extract from an external auditor's report on financial statements.

In our opinion, the financial statements give a true and fair view of the state of the company's affairs as at 31 December 20X2 and of its profit for the year then ended.

▼

Drop-down list:

Absolute assurance
Limited assurance
Reasonable assurance

Task 2 (3 marks)

Below are three statements regarding an external audit of financial statements conducted under International Standards on Auditing (ISAs).

Identify whether each statement is true or false.

Statement	True ✓	False ✓
The external auditor's responsibility is to express an opinion on whether the financial statements are prepared in accordance with an applicable financial reporting framework.		
An external audit provides reasonable assurance on the future viability of the audited entity.		
The application of ISAs requires the external auditor to exercise professional judgement.		

Task 3 (3 marks)

Complete the following statements relating to the external auditor's liability.

The inclusion of a statement disclaiming liability in the external auditor's report may reduce the risk of claims for damages from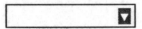

Drop-down list:

shareholders and third parties.
shareholders only.
third parties only.

An agreement that places a limit on the monetary amount of damages payable by the external auditor in the event or professional negligence is known as

Drop-down list:

a liability cap.
professional indemnity insurance.

....

Task 4 (4 marks)

(a) Identify, for each of the descriptions below, the concept it represents.

Not to allow bias, conflict of interest or undue influence of others to override professional or business judgments.

Drop-down list:

Independence
Objectivity

To comply with relevant laws and regulations and avoid any action that discredits the profession.

Drop-down list:

Professional behaviour
Professional competence and due care

160

(b) **Which one of the following situations is likely to give rise to a familiarity threat to independence and objectivity?**

	✓
Performance of both internal and external audit services for an audited entity	
Acting as engagement partner on the audit of a listed entity for more than five years	
The current year's audit is about to commence and the fee from the previous year's audit is still outstanding	

Task 5 (2 marks)

Below are two statements regarding potential safeguards to be applied to protect an external auditor's independence and objectivity.

Identify whether each statement below is true or false.

Statement	True ✓	False ✓
When providing both internal and external audit services to an audited entity, the assurance firm should use different personnel for each of the services.		
The rotation of audit personnel is an appropriate safeguard to mitigate an advocacy threat which has arisen because the assurance firm is acting as an expert witness in support of the client entity.		

Task 6 (3 marks)

There are certain circumstances in which an external auditor must or may disclose confidential information relating to an existing or former client. Some circumstances require the client's permission while others do not.

Identify whether each of the following circumstances requires the external auditor to obtain the client's permission in order to disclose confidential information.

Circumstance	Requires the client's permission ✓	Does NOT require the client's permission ✓
The external auditor suspects that a client is involved in tax evasion.		
A request by a newly-appointed external auditor to access the previous external auditor's working papers, relating to the new client.		
The provision of evidence in the course of legal proceedings.		

Task 7 (3 marks)

When evaluating internal controls at an audited entity, the external auditor needs to understand a number of technical terms.

For each of the descriptions below, identify the technical term to which it relates.

The actions, policies and procedures that reflect the overall attitudes of the management of an entity about control and its importance to the entity.

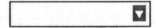

Drop-down list:

Control environment
Risk assessment process

The allocation of responsibilities for authorisation, custody and recording to different personnel.

Drop-down list:

Collusion
Segregation of duties

A function of an entity that performs assurance and consulting activities designed to evaluate and improve the effectiveness of the entity's governance, risk management and internal control processes.

▼

Drop-down list:

External audit
Internal audit

Task 8 (3 marks)

Accounting systems have features such as control objectives and control procedures to mitigate the risk that a control objective is not met.

Identify whether each element below is a control objective, risk or control procedure in respect of the laws and regulations governing an audited entity by dragging the appropriate feature into the table. Each answer option can be used more than once or not at all.

Element	Feature
Exposures to fines and penalties	
Appointment of a compliance officer to monitor operations	
Compliance with industry laws and regulations	

Features:

Control procedure	Control objective	Risk

Task 9 (5 marks)

The internal control checklist for Gita Ltd indicates that a monthly check is conducted of the names on the payroll against the personnel records held by the HR department.

(a) **Identify whether or not this would provide assurance on each of the following control objectives.**

Control objective	Assurance provided ✓	No assurance provided ✓
The payroll is complete and contains the names of all employees.		
The employees on the payroll are genuine employees.		

(b) **Identify whether each of the following procedures within an inventory system is a strength or a deficiency.**

Procedure	Strength ✓	Deficiency ✓
Warehouse staff, who are responsible for the custody and recording of inventory, perform monthly counts of the inventory and check the physical quantities to the inventory records.		
During the year-end physical count, staff are instructed to keep the movement of inventory to a minimum.		
The inventory count sheets distributed to staff responsible for the inventory count include a pre-printed description of each item of inventory and the quantity of each item.		

Task 10 (4 marks)

An entity uses internal control procedures to mitigate the risks to which it is exposed.

Listed below are two internal control procedures which are applicable to an entity's inventory system.

Match each internal control procedure to the risk it mitigates by dragging the appropriate answers into the table.

Internal control procedure	Risk mitigated
All inventory despatched from the warehouse is checked against supporting documentation	
Exception reporting of inventory items which have not moved in three months	

Drag and drop options:

Running out of inventory	Obsolete inventory	Theft of inventory

Task 11 (4 marks)

External auditors use tests of control, tests of detail and analytical procedures to gather audit evidence in respect of financial statement assertions.

(a) **Identify whether the following procedure is a test of control, a test of detail or an analytical procedure.**

Developing an expectation of payroll costs using the average pay per employee multiplied by the number of employees.

[▼]

Drop-down list:

Analytical procedure
Test of control
Test of detail

(b) **Identify the financial statement assertion for which the procedure described below will provide assurance.**

Inspection of the results of the impairment reviews undertaken by the audited entity's management.

[▼]

Task 12 (2 marks)

Two types of computer-assisted audit techniques (CAATs) are test data and audit software.

Identify, for each of the procedures listed below, the type of CAAT that would be used to perform that procedure by selecting the appropriate option.

Procedure	Test data ✓	Audit software ✓
Interrogation of inventory files to identify inventory which has a selling price below its cost		
Input of goods amount and VAT amount on a sales invoice with an incorrect total to check that the system reports the error		

Task 13 (4 marks)

When using sampling techniques in auditing, the external auditor needs to understand a number of technical terms.

(a) Identify the technical term for each of the descriptions below.

A sampling approach whereby a population is divided into two or more subsets which have similar characteristics.

Drop-down list:

Block selection
Stratification

The risk that the auditor misinterprets audit evidence obtained.

Drop-down list:

Non-sampling risk
Sampling risk

When selecting items in order to perform tests of detail, the external auditor has to consider a number of factors.

(b) **Identify whether the following factor will result in an increase in sample size, decrease in sample size or have a negligible effect on sample size.**

An increase in the use of other substantive procedures directed at the same assertion.

Drop-down list:

Decrease in sample size
Increase in sample size
Negligible effect on sample size

Task 14 (3 marks)

The external auditor may adopt an audit approach which involves undertaking either:

- Tests of controls and substantive procedures, or
- Substantive procedures only, with no tests of controls.

Identify the most likely approach to be adopted by the external auditor in each of the following circumstances.

Circumstance	Test of controls and substantive procedures ✓	Substantive procedures only, with no tests of controls ✓
The audited entity introduced a new integrated accounting software package at the beginning of the accounting period and is experiencing operational difficulties with it.		
There is no segregation of duties within the accounting function of the audited entity.		
The audited entity has an internal audit function which routinely monitors operational and financial controls.		

Task 15 (2 marks)

You are responsible for testing that cash sales are fairly stated in the financial statements of Zita Ltd. You are require to test cash sales for both understatement and overstatement.

Identify whether the following audit procedure would test for understatement, overstatement or for both understatement and overstatement of cash sales.

Trace till records to corresponding entries in the cash book.

Drop-down list:

Both understatement and overstatement
Overstatement only
Understatement only

Task 16 (10 marks)

Audit risk is the product of inherent risk, control risk and detection risk. The external auditor assesses inherent and control risk to determine the audit approach. He then manages detection to keep audit risk at an acceptably low level.

(a) **Identify whether each of the following statements, in respect of audit risk and its components, is true or false.**

The susceptibility of an assertion to a misstatement that could be material (either individually or when aggregated with other misstatements) before consideration of any related controls, is known as inherent risk.

Sampling risk and non-sampling risk are components of detection risk.

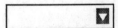

Drop-down list:

True
False

(b) **Identify whether each of the following factors is likely to lead to the auditor assessing control risk as higher or lower.**

Management of the audited entity routinely reviews exception reports of unusual or high-value transactions.

▼

The audited entity has introduced a new computerised accounting system without a parallel run of the old and new systems.

▼

Management of the audited entity does not understand the concept of segregation of duties.

▼

Drop-down list:

Control risk higher
Control risk lower

(c) **Identify whether or not each of the following actions will increase or decrease detection risk.**

A reduction in sample sizes when testing transactions and balances.

▼

The use of an industry expert when assessing impairment reviews undertaken by the audited entity's management.

▼

An increase in the level of professional skepticism.

▼

Drop-down list:

Decrease detection risk
Increase detection risk

The external auditor is required to undertake analytical procedures as part of the planning process to identify the risk of misstatement in the financial statements.

The gross profit margin at Dahlia Ltd, a manufacturing company, has decreased in comparison to the previous year.

(d) **Which one of the following may provide a plausible explanation for the fall in Dahlia's Ltd's gross profit margin?**

▼

Drop-down list:

Overstatement of sales
Understatement of purchases
Understatement of closing work in progress

Task 17 (3 marks)

Identify whether each of the following statements is true or false in respect of materiality.

Statement	True ✓	False ✓
Performance materiality is used at the planning stage of an external audit to determine which items to test.		
Once the materiality threshold has been established at the planning stage of the audit, it should not be revised as the audit progresses.		
Failure by the audited entity to disclose a contingent liability, amounting to 11% of profit before tax and 3% of total assets, in the notes to the financial statements would generally be considered material but not pervasive.		

Task 18 (10 marks)

You are planning the audit of Gear Ltd (Gear), a wholesaler of clothing and fashion accessories that are targeted at the younger market. The company imports all of its goods from manufacturers in the Far East who invoice Gear in US dollars.

The majority of Gear's customers are small independent retailers who are required to pay within 30 days of invoice date. However, a number of these customers are experiencing cash flow problems and their balances have been outstanding for over 90 days.

Gear recently implemented a new computer system. The accounting package was supplied by a software company which had recently commenced trading. The software supplier assisted the company with the changeover from the old to the new system and as a result, management decided that there was no need to involve the external auditor or have a period of parallel running.

Gear's bookkeeper is solely responsible for the input of data, but due to the changeover she is several weeks behind with her work. She plans to catch up by working overtime and hopes to be up to date by the time of the external audit.

Required

Identify and explain the audit risks relating to the external audit of Gear Ltd. Where possible, your answer should refer to specific items in the financial statements which may be at risk of misstatement.

Task 19 (10 marks)

You are the audit senior on the external audit of Engco Ltd (Engco) and are responsible for checking that inventory is fairly stated in the financial statements. Engco assembles engines for tractors from bought-in components, some of which are sourced from overseas suppliers which are paid in their local currency.

Engco maintains a cost record for each model of engine assembled. Each cost record contains the following details:

(a) Components – with their costs

(b) Direct labour – standard time multiplied by hourly rate

(c) Production overheads – calculated as 20% of direct costs. This percentage is based on the percentage of production costs to direct costs in the management accounts.

Engco maintains continuous inventory records, checked by periodic counting for components but not for finished goods (ie assembled engines). Consequently, there is no year-end inventory count for components but there is a year-end count for assembled engines.

Required

Set out, in a manner suitable for inclusion in the audit plan, the audit procedures to be undertaken to ensure that the ASSEMBLED ENGINES are fairly stated in the financial statements for the year ended 31 December 20X2.

Task 20 (3 marks)

Audit documentation serves a number of purposes.

Identify the purpose of each of the working papers in the table below by dragging the appropriate reason for preparation next to each working paper. Each answer option can be used more than once or not at all.

Working paper	Reason for preparation
Details of the physical condition of the audited entity's plant and equipment.	
Independence questionnaire completed by each member of the engagement team	
Copies of cash flow and profit forecasts prepared by the audited entity's management	

Answer options:

Compliance with the ethical	Assess going concern status	Support impairment adjustments

Task 21 (3 marks)

During the audit of Duggan Ltd, the audit junior has identified three journal entries which he considers to be unusual.

Identify whether each of the journal entries listed below should be referred to the audit supervisor.

Journal entry	Refer to supervisor ✓	Do not refer to supervisor ✓
The writing down of an amount relating to an item of inventory which has been damaged.		
The transfer of an amount from repairs and maintenance to cost of property, plant and equipment, which resulted in an increase in profit to the level required for the payment of directors' bonuses.		

Journal entry	Refer to supervisor ✓	Do not refer to supervisor ✓
The writing off as an irrecoverable debt, an amount relating to a loan to the managing director of Duggan Ltd.		

Task 22 (10 marks)

Iceprods Ltd, a wholesaler of frozen foods, is based in the UK. The storage of frozen food is highly regulated in the UK and businesses such as Iceprods Ltd are subject to periodic inspections by the regulator to ensure compliance with hygiene regulations. Iceprods Ltd operates a continuous inventory system, which is checked by monthly counting. During the external audit, it was discovered that no check is made of the sell-by dates of products in inventory and there are no procedures to ensure that older inventory is despatched to customers first.

Required

Prepare extracts, suitable for inclusion in a report to the management of Iceprods Ltd, which set out the following in respect of this matter:

(a) The possible consequences, and

(b) The recommendations you would make.

Task 23 (4 marks)

The two following situations have arisen at two unrelated audit clients.

Identify, for each situation, the type of audit opinion on the financial statements that should be expressed.

The financial statements of Dorratta Ltd include a note regarding a significant uncertainty about the going concern status of the company. The engagement partner is satisfied that the note includes all the necessary disclosures for users of the financial statements to understand the situation.

Drop-down list:

Adverse opinion
Qualified opinion
Unmodified opinion

The external auditor of Garotta Ltd was appointed after the year end and, as a result, was unable to attend the year-end inventory count. Garotta Ltd does not maintain continuous inventory records so the external auditor was unable to perform alternative audit procedures to obtain sufficient appropriate evidence regarding the reliability of the inventory figure in the financial statements.

Drop-down list:

Unmodified opinion
Qualified opinion due to material misstatement
Qualified opinion due to limitation on scope

AAT AQ2016 SAMPLE ASSESSMENT 1
EXTERNAL AUDITING

ANSWERS

External Auditing: AAT sample assessment 1

Task 1 (2 marks)

Identify the level of assurance provided by the following extract from an external auditor's report on financial statements.

In our opinion, the financial statements give a true and fair view of the state of the company's affairs as at 31 December 20X2 and of its profit for the year then ended.

Reasonable assurance

Task 2 (3 marks)

Below are three statements regarding an external audit of financial statements conducted under International Standards on Auditing (ISAs).

Identify whether each statement is true or false.

Statement	True ✓	False ✓
The external auditor's responsibility is to express an opinion on whether the financial statements are prepared in accordance with an applicable financial reporting framework.	✓	
An external audit provides reasonable assurance on the future viability of the audited entity.		✓
The application of ISAs requires the external auditor to exercise professional judgement.	✓	

Task 3 (3 marks)

Complete the following statements relating to the external auditor's liability.

The inclusion of a statement disclaiming liability in the external auditor's report may reduce the risk of claims for damages from $\boxed{\text{third parties only.}}$

An agreement that places a limit on the monetary amount of damages payable by the external auditor in the event or professional negligence is known as

$\boxed{\text{a liability cap.}}$

Task 4 (4 marks)

(a) Identify, for each of the descriptions below, the concept it represents.

Not to allow bias, conflict of interest or undue influence of others to override professional or business judgments.

$\boxed{\text{Objectivity}}$

To comply with the relevant laws and regulations and avoid any action that discredits the profession.

$\boxed{\text{Professional behaviour}}$

(b) Which one of the following situations is likely to give rise to a familiarity threat to independence and objectivity?

	✓
Performance of both internal and external audit services for an audited entity	
Acting as engagement partner on the audit of a listed entity for more than five years	✓
The current year's audit is about to commence and the fee from the previous year's audit is still outstanding	

Task 5 (2 marks)

Below are two statements regarding potential safeguards to be applied to protect an external auditor's independence and objectivity.

Identify whether each statement below is true or false.

Statement	True ✓	False ✓
When providing both internal and external audit services to an audited entity, the assurance firm should use different personnel for each of the services.	✓	
The rotation of audit personnel is an appropriate safeguard to mitigate an advocacy threat which has arisen because the assurance firm is acting as an expert witness in support of the client entity.		✓

Task 6 (3 marks)

There are certain circumstances in which an external auditor must or may disclose confidential information relating to an existing or former client. Some circumstances require the client's permission while others do not.

Identify whether each of the following circumstances requires the external auditor to obtain the client's permission in order to disclose confidential information.

Circumstance	Requires the client's permission ✓	Does NOT require the client's permission ✓
The external auditor suspects that a client is involved in tax evasion.		✓
A request by a newly-appointed external auditor to access the previous external auditor's working papers, relating to the new client.	✓	
The provision of evidence in the course of legal proceedings.		✓

Task 7 (3 marks)

When evaluating internal controls at an audited entity, the external auditor needs to understand a number of technical terms.

For each of the descriptions below, identify the technical term to which it relates.

The actions, policies and procedures that reflect the overall attitudes of the management of an entity about control and its importance to the entity.

> Control environment

The allocation of responsibilities for authorisation, custody and recording to different personnel.

> Segregation of duties

A function of an entity that performs assurance and consulting activities designed to evaluate and improve the effectiveness of the entity's governance, risk management and internal control processes.

> Internal audit

Task 8 (3 marks)

Accounting systems have features such as control objectives and control procedures to mitigate the risk that a control objective is not met.

Identify whether each element below is a control objective, risk or control procedure in respect of the laws and regulations governing an audited entity by dragging the appropriate feature into the table. Each answer option can be used more than once or not at all.

Element	Feature
Exposures to fines and penalties	Risk
Appointment of a compliance officer to monitor operations	Control procedure
Compliance with industry laws and regulations	Control objective

Task 9 (5 marks)

The internal control checklist for Gita Ltd indicates that a monthly check is conducted of the names on the payroll against the personnel records held by the HR department.

(a) **Identify whether or not this would provide assurance on each of the following control objectives.**

Control objective	Assurance provided ✓	No assurance provided ✓
The payroll is complete and contains the names of all employees.		✓
The employees on the payroll are genuine employees.	✓	

(b) **Identify whether each of the following procedures within an inventory system is a strength or a deficiency.**

Procedure	Strength ✓	Deficiency ✓
Warehouse staff, who are responsible for the custody and recording of inventory, perform monthly counts of the inventory and check the physical quantities to the inventory records.		✓
During the year-end physical count, staff are instructed to keep the movement of inventory to a minimum.	✓	
The inventory count sheets distributed to staff responsible for the inventory count include a pre-printed description of each item of inventory and the quantity of each item.		✓

Task 10 (4 marks)

An entity uses internal control procedures to mitigate the risks to which it is exposed.

Listed below are two internal control procedures which are applicable to an entity's inventory system.

Match each internal control procedure to the risk it mitigates by dragging the appropriate answers into the table.

Internal control procedure	Risk mitigated
All inventory despatched from the warehouse is checked against supporting documentation	Theft of inventory
Exception reporting of inventory items which have not moved in three months	Obsolete inventory

Task 11 (4 marks)

External auditors use tests of control, tests of detail and analytical procedures to gather audit evidence in respect of financial statement assertions.

(a) Identify whether the following procedure is a test of control, a test of detail or an analytical procedure.

Developing an expectation of payroll costs using the average pay per employee multiplied by the number of employees.

Analytical procedure

(b) Identify the financial statement assertion for which the procedure described below will provide assurance.

Inspection of the results of the impairment reviews undertaken by the audited entity's management.

Accuracy, valuation and allocation

Task 12 (2 marks)

Two types of computer-assisted audit techniques (CAATs) are test data and audit software.

Identify, for each of the procedures listed below, the type of CAAT that would be used to perform that procedure by selecting the appropriate option.

Procedure	Test data ✓	Audit software ✓
Interrogation of inventory files to identify inventory which has a selling price below its cost		✓
Input of goods amount and VAT amount on a sales invoice with an incorrect total to check that the system reports the error	✓	

Task 13 (4 marks)

When using sampling techniques in auditing, the external auditor needs to understand a number of technical terms.

(a)   Identify the technical term for each of the descriptions below.

A sampling approach whereby a population is divided into two or more subsets which have similar characteristics.

Stratification

The risk that the auditor misinterprets audit evidence obtained.

Non-sampling risk

When selecting items in order to perform tests of detail, the external auditor has to consider a number of factors.

(b)   Identify whether the following factor will result in an increase in sample size, decrease in sample size or have a negligible effect on sample size.

An increase in the use of other substantive procedures directed at the same assertion.

Decrease in sample size

Task 14 (3 marks)

The external auditor may adopt an audit approach which involves undertaking either:

(a)   Tests of controls and substantive procedures, or

(b)   Substantive procedures only, with no tests of controls

Identify the most likely approach to be adopted by the external auditor in each of the following circumstances.

Circumstance	Test of controls and substantive procedures ✓	Substantive procedures only, with no tests of controls ✓
The audited entity introduced a new integrated accounting software package at the beginning of the accounting period and is experiencing operational difficulties with it.		✓
There is no segregation of duties within the accounting function of the audited entity.		✓
The audited entity has an internal audit function which routinely monitors operational and financial controls.	✓	

Task 15 (2 marks)

You are responsible for testing that cash sales are fairly stated in the financial statements of Zita Ltd. You are require to test cash sales for both understatement and overstatement.

Identify whether the following audit procedure would test for understatement, overstatement or for both understatement and overstatement of cash sales.

Trace till records to corresponding entries in the cash book.

Understatement only

Task 16 (10 marks)

Audit risk is the product of inherent risk, control risk and detection risk. The external auditor assesses inherent and control risk to determine the audit approach. He then manages detection to keep audit risk at an acceptably low level.

(a) **Identify whether each of the following statements, in respect of audit risk and its components, is true or false.**

The susceptibility of an assertion to a misstatement that could be material (either individually or when aggregated with other misstatements) before consideration of any related controls, is known as inherent risk.

> True

Sampling risk and non-sampling risk are components of detection risk.

> True

(b) **Identify whether each of the following factors is likely to lead to the auditor assessing control risk as higher or lower.**

Management of the audited entity routinely reviews exception reports of unusual or high-value transactions.

> Control risk lower

The audited entity has introduced a new computerised accounting system without a parallel run of the old and new systems.

> Control risk higher

Management of the audited entity does not understand the concept of segregation of duties.

> Control risk higher

(c) **Identify whether or not each of the following actions will increase or decrease detection risk.**

A reduction in sample sizes when testing transactions and balances.

> Increase detection risk

The use of an industry expert when assessing impairment reviews undertaken by the audited entity's management.

> Decrease detection risk

An increase in the level of professional scepticism.

> Decrease detection risk

The external auditor is required to undertake analytical procedures as part of the planning process to identify the risk of misstatement in the financial statements.

The gross profit margin at Dahlia Ltd, a manufacturing company, has decreased in comparison to the previous year.

(d) **Which one of the following may provide a plausible explanation for the fall in Dahlia's Ltd's gross profit margin?**

> Understatement of closing work in progress

Task 17 (3 marks)

Identify whether each of the following statements is true or false in respect of materiality.

Statement	True ✓	False ✓
Performance materiality is used at the planning stage of an external audit to determine which items to test.	✓	
Once the materiality threshold has been established at the planning stage of the audit, it should not be revised as the audit progresses.		✓
Failure by the audited entity to disclose a contingent liability, amounting to 11% of profit before tax and 3% of total assets, in the notes to the financial statements would generally be considered material but not pervasive.	✓	

Task 18 (10 marks)

Identify and explain the audit risks relating to the external audit of Gear Ltd. Where possible, your answer should refer to specific items in the financial statements which may be at risk of misstatement.

Fashion goods:

- Subject to obsolescence
- NRV may be lower than cost
- Inventory may be overstated

Clothing and accessories paid for in US dollars:

Risk of inappropriate exchange rates/translation errors in:

- Purchases
- Payables
- Inventory

Overdue receivables:

- Potential irrecoverable debts
- Overstated receivables and profit
- Understated allowances for doubtful debts

New computer system:

Increased risk of errors due to:

- Lack of familiarity
- Lack of parallel running
- Unproven track record of software company
- Lack of external auditor involvement

Backlog of work:

- Increased risk of errors
- In particular, risk of cut-off errors at year end

Bookkeeper solely responsible for input of data:

- Lack of segregation of duties
- Increased risk of misstatement due to fraud or error

Task 19 (10 marks)

Set out, in a manner suitable for inclusion in the audit plan, the audit procedures to be undertaken to ensure that the ASSEMBLED ENGINES are fairly stated in the financial statements for the year ended 31 December 20X2.

Attend the year-end inventory count

Evaluate procedures, in particular:

- Counting in pairs
- Use of sequentially numbered count sheets
- Independent supervision
- Marking items once counted
- Movements kept to a minimum
- Damaged items noted

Perform test counts:

- Floor to sheet
- Sheet to floor

For a sample of cost records:

- Vouch component costs back to purchase invoices

- Re-perform translations from foreign currency and

- Check the exchange rate to a reliable source

- Ensure completeness of included components by discussion with employees

- Check the time taken to assemble by observation/discussion with employees/timesheets

- Vouch hourly rate to payroll records

- Re-perform the overhead calculation and ensure

  - = 20% of direct costs

  - production costs per management accounts/direct costs per management accounts = 20%

- Ensure overheads are productive in nature/no selling or administrative costs included

- Ensure overheads based on normal level of activity/enquire into any idle time

Review selling prices after year end to ensure above cost

Review movements after year end to identify slow-moving/obsolete items

Task 20 (3 marks)

Audit documentation serves a number of purposes.

Identify the purpose of each of the working papers in the table below by dragging the appropriate reason for preparation next to each working paper. Each answer option can be used more than once or not at all.

Working paper	Reason for preparation
Details of the physical condition of the audited entity's plant and equipment.	Support impairment adjustments
Independence questionnaire completed by each member of the engagement team	Compliance with the ethical requirements
Copies of cash flow and profit forecasts prepared by the audited entity's management	Assess going concern status

Task 21 (3 marks)

During the audit of Duggan Ltd, the audit junior has identified three journal entries which he considers to be unusual.

Identify whether each of the journal entries listed below should be referred to the audit supervisor.

Journal entry	Refer to supervisor ✓	Do not refer to supervisor ✓
The writing down of an amount relating to an item of inventory which has been damaged.		✓
The transfer of an amount from repairs and maintenance to cost of property, plant and equipment, which resulted in an increase in profit to the level required for the payment of directors' bonuses.	✓	
The writing off as an irrecoverable debt, an amount relating to a loan to the managing director of Duggan Ltd.	✓	

Task 22 (10 marks)

Prepare extracts, suitable for inclusion in a report to the management of Iceprods Ltd, which set out the following in respect of this matter:

(a) The possible consequences, and

(b) The recommendations you would make.

(a) Consequences

- Obsolete inventory
- Costs incurred if products have to be scrapped/destroyed
- Adverse impact on cash flow
- Adverse impact on profits
- Expired products may be sold
- Leading to loss of customer goodwill/business
- Or food poisoning
- Giving rise to legal claims
- Investigated by Regulator (Environmental Health), resulting in
    - fines, or
    - possible closure.

(b) Recommendations

(i) Specific

- Regular checks of sell-by dates to be made during inventory counts
- Introduce process in warehouse to ensure inventory despatched on a FIFO basis
- Record sell-by dates on inventory system and regularly check not expired
- Check dates on all products before despatched to customers

    Expired inventory should be immediately destroyed

    Exception reporting of items close to sell-by date

- Discount items approaching sell-by date in order to sell inventory with short life

(ii) General

- Communicate policy to staff/train staff
- Monitor procedures to ensure compliance
- Disciplinary procedures for failing to comply with company policy

Task 23 (4 marks)

The two following situations have arisen at two unrelated audit clients.

Identify, for each situation, the type of audit opinion on the financial statements that should be expressed.

The financial statements of Dorratta Ltd include a note regarding a significant uncertainty about the going concern status of the company. The engagement partner is satisfied that the note includes all the necessary disclosures for users of the financial statements to understand the situation.

Unmodified opinion

The external auditor of Garotta Ltd was appointed after the year end and, as a result, was unable to attend the year-end inventory count. Garotta Ltd does not maintain continuous inventory records so the external auditor was unable to perform alternative audit procedures to obtain sufficient appropriate evidence regarding the reliability of the inventory figure in the financial statements.

Qualified opinion due to limitation on scope

AAT AQ2016 SAMPLE ASSESSMENT 2 EXTERNAL AUDITING

You are advised to attempt sample assessment 2 online from the AAT website. This will ensure you are prepared for how the assessment will be presented on the AAT's system when you attempt the real assessment. Please access the assessment using the address below:

https://www.aat.org.uk/training/study-support/search

BPP PRACTICE ASSESSMENT 1
EXTERNAL AUDITING

Time allowed: 2 hours

External Auditing: BPP practice assessment 1

Task 1

Identify whether the sentence below is a definition of reasonable or limited assurance by selecting the appropriate option.

A high, but not absolute, level of assurance.	▼

Picklist:

Limited assurance
Reasonable assurance

Task 2

Identify whether the following statements in respect of auditors' and directors' duties are true or false.

	True ✓	False ✓
UK auditors are required to follow the guidance of International Standards on Auditing (ISAs) issued by the International Audit and Assurance Board (IAASB) and adapted by the Financial Reporting Council (FRC).		
Adequate accounting records means records that are sufficient to show and explain the company's transactions during the financial year.		
Adequate accounting records means records that are sufficient to enable the Directors to show with reasonable accuracy at the year-end only the financial position of the company at that time.		

Task 3

Which of the following best describes audit failure? Select all that apply.

	✓
Audits resulting in the auditors being found guilty of negligence.	
Audits resulting in a modified auditor's report.	
Audits failing to uncover a fraud perpetrated by the managing director.	
Audits resulting in a qualified audit opinion	

Task 4

(a) Identify, for each of the descriptions below, the concept it represents.

A member shall act diligently and in accordance with applicable technical and professional standards when providing professional services.

Picklist:

Professional behaviour
Professional competence and due care

To be straightforward and honest in all professional and business relationships.

Picklist:

Integrity
Objectivity

(b) **Which one of the following situations is likely to give rise to a self-review threat to independence and objectivity?**

	✓
Undue dependence on total fees from a client.	
Potential employment with a client.	
Reporting on the operation of financial systems after being involved in their design or implementation.	

Task 5

Below are two statements regarding potential safeguards to be applied to protect an external auditor's independence and objectivity.

Identify whether each statement is true or false.

	True ✓	False ✓
When providing information technology services to an audited entity, the assurance firm can use the same personnel for both services.		
Changing employment from the assurance firm to a client can lead to the need for an independent review of their work.		

Task 6

There are certain circumstances in which an external auditor must or may disclose confidential information relating to an existing or former client. Some circumstances require the client's permission while others do not.

Identify whether each of the following circumstances requires the external auditor to obtain the client's permission in order the disclose confidential information.

	Requires the client's permission ✓	Does NOT require the client's permission ✓
During the audit of Gala Ltd, the audit senior discovered that the purchases director accepts bonuses from suppliers for using them. Discussion with personnel in the personal tax department revealed that these bonuses do not appear on the director's personal tax return.		
The Financial Reporting Council has asked your firm to supply details of the audit of Regatta Ltd as part of its ongoing quality control procedures.		
The audit manager has requested the outgoing external auditor's working papers for review as part of planning the recently commenced audit of Festival Ltd.		

Task 7

Complete the following definitions relating to internal controls, by selecting the appropriate option from the picklist below.

The control [_____▼] includes the governance and management functions, and the attitudes, awareness and actions of directors and management concerning the entity's internal control and its importance in the entity.

Control [_____▼] are policies and procedures established to achieve the entity's specific objectives.

[_____▼] of controls is a process to assess the quality of internal control performance over time.

Picklist:

Actions
Activities
Environment
Monitoring
Objectives
Planning

Task 8

Accounting systems have features such as control objectives and control procedures to mitigate the risks that a control objective is not met.

Identify whether each of the following is a control objective, risk or control procedure by selecting the appropriate option.

Order forms are pre-numbered.	▼
Orders are only taken when current account balances have been checked.	▼
Orders may not be recorded.	▼

Picklist:

Control objective
Control procedure
Risk

Task 9

An external auditor is required to obtain an understanding of the control environment within an audited entity.

(a) **Identify whether the following factors contribute to a strong control environment, a weak control environment or have no effect by selecting the appropriate option.**

A company's staff is competent and acts with integrity.	▼
The directors assess fraud and compliance risks on a monthly basis.	▼

Picklist:

No effect
Strong
Weak

External auditors use a variety of methods for documenting systems of control, including flowcharts, internal control questionnaires and narrative notes.

(b) **Identify for each of the following situations the method which seems most appropriate by selecting the relevant option.**

It is a new client. The audit manager wants a comprehensive description of the complex system before it is evaluated.	▼
It is an existing client. The auditors have always relied on controls, but management has recently overhauled the controls system in an attempt to make cost savings. The audit manager is keen to ensure that the new system is capable of mitigating control risk.	▼

Picklist:

Flowchart
Internal control questionnaire
Narrative notes

The following are descriptions of procedures within the sales system of New Jersey Ltd.

(c) **For each procedure, identify whether it is a strength or a deficiency, by selecting the appropriate option.**

Procedure	Strength or deficiency
Jane is in charge of invoice processing and Amelia is in charge of cash receipts.	▾
Amelia banks cash receipts once a week.	▾

Picklist:

Deficiency
Strength

Task 10

An entity uses internal control procedures in order to mitigate the risks to which the entity is exposed. Listed below are two internal control procedures which are applicable to an entity's non-current asset procurement system.

Match each risk mitigated to the internal control procedure by completing the table with the appropriate risk to the procedures.

Internal control procedure	Risk mitigated
Monthly capital expenditure budget prepared.	▾
Capital expenditure purchase orders approved at monthly directors' meetings.	▾

Picklist:

Assets paid for when not received
Assets purchased for personal use
Company buys assets at the best price
Company does not have access to appropriate assets when required

Task 11

Auditors use tests of control and substantive procedures to gather audit evidence.

Identify, for each of the procedures below, whether it is a test of control or a substantive procedure by selecting the appropriate option.

	Test of control ✓	Substantive procedure ✓
Inspection of reconciliation between purchase ledger and supplier statement.		
Reconciliation of purchase ledger balance to supplier statement.		
Comparison of year end payables balance with prior year payables balance.		

Task 12

Identify whether the following statements in respect of Computer Assisted Audit Techniques (CAATs) are true or false, by selecting the appropriate option.

	True ✓	False ✓
Auditors may use test data in which they process false data to ensure that the system rejects it.		
Auditors may use test data to compare data on personnel and payroll master files to ensure consistency.		

Task 13

When using sampling techniques in auditing, the external auditor needs to understand a number of technical terms.

(a) Select the most appropriate technical term that is used for the following description.

Description	Technical term
The external auditor selects a sample from the population but accepts that the sample may not be fully representative of that population.	▼

Picklist:

Detection risk
Non-sampling risk
Sampling risk

When selecting items to in order to perform tests of detail, the auditor has to consider a number of factors.

(b) Identify, for each of the following factors, the impact they will have on sample size, by selecting the appropriate option.

Factor	Impact on sample size
Increase in tolerable misstatement	▼
Increase in expected misstatement	▼
Increase in number of sampling units	▼

Picklist:

Decrease
Increase
No effect

Task 14

The external auditor may adopt an audit approach which involves undertaking either:

(a) Tests of controls and substantive procedures, or
(b) Substantive procedures only, with no tests of control.

Identify the most likely approach to be adopted by the external auditor in each of the following circumstances.

Circumstance	Tests of controls and substantive procedures ✓	Substantive procedures with no tests of controls ✓
New members of the accounting team are given a controls manual, and where possible, asked to shadow their predecessor to learn the relevant controls for their position.		
Control activities are reviewed on an annual basis after the annual audit, and improvements made if seen fit.		
No member of the accounts team has any formal accountancy training, and prior year files show that audit recommendations relating to controls are not implemented.		

Task 15

As part of verification techniques in respect of non-current assets, an auditor is going to inspect hire purchase agreements. The auditor will gain assurance about different assertions depending on the information on the agreements.

In respect of the information below, select the assertion for which that information will provide primary assurance.

Information	Assertion
Description of the agreement entered into	▾
Contract price	▾

Picklist:

Accuracy, valuation and allocation
Completeness
Existence
Rights and obligations

Task 16

When planning an audit of financial statements, the external auditor is required to consider how factors such as the entity's operating environment and its system of internal control affect the risk of misstatement in the financial statements.

(a) **Identify whether the following factors are likely to increase or reduce the risk of misstatement or have no effect, by selecting the appropriate option.**

Directors communicate and enforce integrity and ethical values.	▼
Top managers are offered profit related bonuses, which are scaled according to the level of profit achieved.	▼
The entity has not taken any action about matters raised in the report to management from the previous three audits.	▼

Picklist:

Increase
No effect
Reduce

The external auditor assesses control risk in order to determine the audit approach.

(b) **Identify, for each of the following factors, whether it is likely to lead to the auditor assessing that there is an increase or a decrease in control risk, by selecting the appropriate option.**

Factor	Increase or decrease in risk
The framework within which an entity's activities for achieving its objectives are planned, executed, controlled and reviewed.	▼
There is a large staff in the accounting department, and key areas are segregated between different staff.	▼
Financial statements are produced by the financial controller after he has carried out a large number of journals to get things in order.	▼

Picklist:

Decrease
Increase

The external auditor is required to undertake analytical procedures as part of the planning process in order to identify the risk of misstatement of figures in the financial statements. The results of analytical procedures conducted on non-current assets are shown below.

(c) **Identify whether the results indicate that non-current assets might have been under or overstated, by selecting the appropriate option.**

The results show that:	
Non-current assets cost has increased by 5%, while the directors claim that there have been no additions to non-current assets.	▼
The repairs and maintenance cost is usually about 3% of total non-current assets. This year it was 25%.	▼

Picklist:

Overstated
Understated

Task 17

Identify whether each of the following statements is true or false in respect of materiality.

Statement	True ✓	False ✓
A percentage guide for materiality is often used, for example 5% of profits.		
An item that results in a modification to the auditor's opinion is always referred to as 'material and pervasive'.		
Performance materiality is the amount or amounts set by the auditor at more than materiality for the financial statements as a whole to reduce to an appropriately low level the probability that the aggregate of uncorrected and undetected misstatements exceeds materiality for the financial statements as a whole.		

Task 18

During the year ended 30 June 20X2, Carling Ltd entered an agreement with a customer, Beck, to allow Carling to store Carling's products at Beck's premises. Beck customers sells the goods to other parties. Carling only accounts for a sale to Beck when Beck has arranged a sale to a third party.

Required

Set out, in a manner suitable for inclusion in the audit plan:

(a) **The audit risks relating to inventory resulting from this agreement.**

(b) **The procedures to be taken to ensure that inventory is fairly stated in the financial statements.**

Task 19

You are planning the audit of receivables at Girlco Ltd. Girlco is an established client, and you attended the previous audit. Girlco has a large sales ledger and there is a high sample size for the audit of receivables. In previous years, customers have not been circularised and the client has requested that you do not circularise customers. Receivables is considered to be low risk, as customers usually pay promptly. This year, Girlco has had a long running dispute with one customer, Ravenna Ltd, about the quality of goods supplied. Ravenna is threatening to find another supplier if the quality problems are not resolved soon.

Required

Set out, in a manner suitable for inclusion in the audit plan, the audit procedures to be undertaken in order to ensure that the receivables balance is fairly stated in the financial statements.

Task 20

Identify whether the following statements in respect of an external auditor's working papers are true or false by selecting the appropriate option.

Auditors are not legally required to maintain working papers.	▼
Working papers give evidence of whether audit work was carried out in line with auditing standards.	▼
Working papers should be labelled with who prepared and who reviewed the working paper, and when those actions were carried out.	▼

Picklist:

True
False

Task 21

In each of the following situations, identify whether or not they should be referred to the audit supervisor.

Situation	Refer to supervisor ✓	Do not refer to supervisor ✓
During the audit of Trout Ltd for the year ended 31 December 20X1, the audit junior identified three instances of sales receipts being posted to the wrong ledger account. The sample was extended, and the control fault found to be isolated. Discussion with client staff indicated all three errors occurred in one week in August, when the sales ledger clerk was on holiday.		
During the audit of HeartCo Ltd, the audit junior identified that the company had purchased a new car in the year which is for the sole use of the managing director's wife, who does not work in the business. The value of the car has been verified to invoice, and it is being depreciated in line with other company cars, over four years.		
A sales invoice for £50 which has been mis-posted between customer accounts on the sales ledger.		

Task 22

During the audit of Smartco Ltd it was discovered that warehouse staff agree delivery documentation against a purchase order when items are delivered (if such delivery documentation exists), sign the document, one part of which is returned to the supplier and the other of which is filed with the purchase order in the warehouse office.

Required

Prepare extracts, suitable for inclusion in a report to management of Smartco Ltd, which set out

(a) **The possible consequences, and**

(b) **The recommendations that you would make in respect of this matter.**

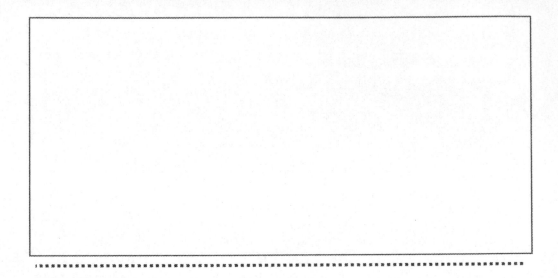

Task 23

For each of the following situations which have arisen in two unrelated audit clients, select the most appropriate form of auditor's opinion for the financial statements.

Materiality is assessed at 5% of profit before tax.

Helena Ltd has profit before tax of £140,000. The directors have included in trade receivables a debt of £9,000. The customer has recently gone into administration. There are no other uncorrected misstatements.	▼
There was a flood at Douglas Ltd and several sales invoice files were destroyed. A copy of the sales invoice is matched with the goods despatched form and kept in the unaffected warehouse stores for 12 months.	▼

Picklist:

Qualified opinion – insufficient inappropriate audit evidence
Qualified opinion – material misstatement
Unmodified opinion only
Unmodified opinion with emphasis of matter paragraph

BPP PRACTICE ASSESSMENT 1
EXTERNAL AUDITING

ANSWERS

External Auditing: BPP practice assessment 1

Task 1

A high, but not absolute, level of assurance.	Reasonable assurance

Task 2

	True ✓	False ✓
UK auditors are required to follow the guidance of International Standards on Auditing (ISAs) issued by the International Audit and Assurance Board (IAASB) and adapted by the Financial Reporting Council (FRC).	✓	
Adequate accounting records means records that are sufficient to show and explain the company's transactions during the financial year.	✓	
Adequate accounting records means records that are sufficient to enable the Directors to show with reasonable accuracy at the year-end only the financial position of the company at that time.		✓

Directors are required to show the financial position **at any time** not just at the year-end.

Task 3

	✓
Audits resulting in the auditors being found guilty of negligence.	✓
Audits resulting in a modified auditor's report.	
Audits failing to uncover a fraud perpetrated by the managing director.	
Audits resulting in a qualified audit opinion	

Although auditors must plan and perform audits with an expectation of discovering fraud causing material misstatement, an MD is in a position to conceal fraudulent activity and an adequately performed audit might not uncover such a fraud.

Modified reports and qualified audit opinions are legitimate outcomes of a quality audit.

Task 4

(a) A member shall act diligently and in accordance with applicable technical and professional standards when providing professional services.

> Professional competence and due care

To be straightforward and honest in all professional and business relationships.

> Integrity

(b)

Undue dependence on total fees from a client.	
Potential employment with a client.	
Reporting on the operation of financial systems after being involved in their design or implementation.	✓

Task 5

	True ✓	False ✓
When providing information technology services to an audited entity, the assurance firm can use the same personnel for both services.		✓
Changing employment from the assurance firm to a client can lead to the need for an independent review of their work.	✓	

Task 6

	Requires the client's permission ✓	Does NOT require the client's permission ✓
During the audit of Gala Ltd, the audit senior discovered that the purchases director accepts bonuses from suppliers for using them. Discussion with personnel in the personal tax department revealed that these bonuses do not appear on the director's personal tax return.		✓
The Financial Reporting Council has asked your firm to supply details of the audit of Regatta Ltd as part of its ongoing quality control procedures.		✓
The audit manager has requested the outgoing external auditor's working papers for review as part of planning the recently commenced audit of Festival Ltd.	✓	

Task 7

The control ⎡ environment ⎤ includes the governance and management functions, and the attitudes, awareness and actions of directors and management concerning the entity's internal control and its importance in the entity.

Control ⎡ activities ⎤ are policies and procedures established to achieve the entity's specific objectives.

⎡ Monitoring ⎤ of controls is a process to assess the quality of internal control over time.

Task 8

Order forms are pre-numbered.	Control procedure
Orders are only taken when current account balances have been checked.	Control procedure
Orders may not be recorded.	Risk

Task 9

(a)

A company's staff is competent and acts with integrity.	No effect – Competent staff may be indicative of a good control environment, but does not contribute to it. The control environment relates to the actions, awareness and attitude of **management** and **those charged with governance**.
The directors assess fraud and compliance risks on a monthly basis.	Strong

(b)

It is a new client. The audit manager wants a comprehensive description of the complex system before it is evaluated.	Narrative notes – It is a complex system so flowchart inappropriate. An ICQ evaluates and records.
It is an existing client. The auditors have always relied on controls, but management has recently overhauled the controls system in an attempt to make cost savings. The audit manager is keen to ensure that the new system is capable of mitigating control risk.	Internal control questionnaire

(c)

Procedure	Strength or deficiency
Jane is in charge of invoice processing and Amelia is in charge of cash receipts.	Strength – Indicates segregation of duties.
Amelia banks cash receipts once a week.	Deficiency – Cash should be banked more frequently if possible.

Task 10

Internal control procedure	Risk mitigated
Monthly capital expenditure budget prepared.	Company does not have access to appropriate assets when required
Capital expenditure purchase orders approved at monthly directors' meetings.	Assets purchased for personal use

Task 11

	Test of control ✓	Substantive procedure ✓
Inspection of reconciliation between purchase ledger and supplier statement.	✓	
Reconciliation of purchase ledger balance to supplier statement.		✓
Comparison of year end payables balance with prior year payables balance.		✓

Task 12

	True ✓	False ✓
Auditors may use test data in which they process false data to ensure that the system rejects it.	✓	
Auditors may use test data to compare data on personnel and payroll master files to ensure consistency.		✓

Task 13

(a)

Description	Technical term
The external auditor selects a sample from the population but accepts that the sample may not be fully representative of that population.	Sampling risk

(b)

Factor	Impact on sample size
Increase in tolerable misstatement	Decrease
Increase in expected misstatement	Increase
Increase in number of sampling units	No effect

Task 14

Circumstance	Tests of controls and substantive procedures ✓	Substantive procedures with no tests of controls ✓
New members of the accounting team are given a controls manual, and where possible, asked to shadow their predecessor to learn the relevant controls for their position.	✓	
Control activities are reviewed on an annual basis after the annual audit, and improvements made if seen fit.	✓	
No member of the accounts team has any formal accountancy training, and prior year files show that audit recommendations relating to controls are not implemented.		✓

Task 15

Information	Assertion
Description of the agreement entered into	Rights and obligations
Contract price	Accuracy, valuation and allocation

Task 16

(a)

Directors communicate and enforce integrity and ethical values.	Reduce
Top managers are offered profit related bonuses, which are scaled according to the level of profit achieved.	Increase
The entity has not taken any action about matters raised in the report to management from the previous three audits.	Increase

(b)

Factor	Increase or decrease in risk
The framework within which an entity's activities for achieving its objectives are planned, executed, controlled and reviewed.	Decrease
There is a large staff in the accounting department, and key areas are segregated between different staff.	Decrease
Financial statements are produced by the financial controller after he has carried out a large number of journals to get things in order.	Increase

(c)

The results show that:	
Non-current assets cost has increased by 5%, while the directors claim that there have been no additions to non-current assets.	Overstated – Cost can only increase by additions
The repairs and maintenance cost is usually about 3% of total non-current assets. This year it was 25%.	Understated – A capital item may have been expensed in repairs and maintenance.

Task 17

Statement	True ✓	False ✓
A percentage guide for materiality is often used, for example 5% of profits.	✓	
An item that results in a modification to the auditor's opinion is always referred to as 'material and pervasive'.		✓ Not always – items that are material but not pervasive can also lead to a modified auditor's opinion.

Statement	True ✓	False ✓
Performance materiality is the amount or amounts set by the auditor at more than materiality for the financial statements as a whole to reduce to an appropriately low level the probability that the aggregate of uncorrected and undetected misstatements exceeds materiality for the financial statements as a whole.		✓ Performance materiality is set at a level lower than materiality

Task 18

(a)   Audit risks

- There is a risk that inventory will be wrongly excluded or included in the financial statements due to confusion over who owns the inventory at the critical time.

- There is an increase in detection risk as the auditor now has another venue to consider when carrying out the inventory count.

(b)   Procedures

- Review terms of the contract to understand the agreement between the parties.

- Attend third party premises on day of inventory count and ascertain if inventory is suitably isolated and cut off procedures exist/operate adequately.

- Confirm inventory held with third party in writing.

- Perform cut off tests between sales by (and therefore to) the third party and inventory in count.

Note. Based on the information available at the time this book was written, we anticipate a task like this would be human marked in the real assessment.

Task 19

- Obtain sales ledger print out showing sales receipts after the year end

- Vouch sales receipts after the year end for a sample of accounts to after date bank statements to ensure account balances are cleared systematically (ie oldest first)

- Perform analytical procedures on sales ledger balances compared to previous year (in particular focus on Ravenna balance)

- Scrutinise sales ledger for old balances (particularly on Ravenna balance)

- Discuss allowance for doubtful debts with credit controller and assess if appropriate

- Review correspondence with Ravenna to assess likelihood of any outstanding balance being paid

Note. Based on the information available at the time this book was written, we anticipate a task like this would be human marked in the real assessment.

Task 20

Auditors are not legally required to maintain working papers.	True
Working papers give evidence of whether audit work was carried out in line with auditing standards.	True
Working papers should be labelled with who prepared and who reviewed the working paper, and when those actions were carried out.	True

Task 21

Situation	Refer to supervisor ✓	Do not refer to supervisor ✓
During the audit of Trout Ltd for the year ended 31 December 20X1, the audit junior identified three instances of sales receipts being posted to the wrong ledger account. The sample was extended, and the control fault found to be isolated. Discussion with client staff indicated all three errors occurred in one week in August, when the sales ledger clerk was on holiday.		✓
During the audit of HeartCo Ltd, the audit junior identified that the company had purchased a new car in the year which is for the sole use of the managing director's wife, who does not work in the business. The value of the car has been verified to invoice, and it is being depreciated in line with other company cars, over four years.	✓	
A sales invoice for £50 which has been mis-posted between customer accounts on the sales ledger.		✓

Task 22

(a) **Consequences:**

(i) If delivery documentation is not provided by the supplier, it is possible no check is made on what the delivery is.

(ii) No check is made on whether the delivery matches the documentation.

(iii) No check is made on whether the goods are a suitable quality/state to be accepted by the business.

(iv) No link appears to be made between goods being received in the warehouse and invoices being received in the accounts department.

(b) **Recommendations:**

(i) The items delivered should be checked to the delivery documentation and the order in terms of quantity and quality before the goods (and by implication, the liability in respect of them) are accepted and signed for.

(ii) Ideally, an internal goods received note (GRN) should be raised.

(iii) Any issues should be noted on the delivery documentation and a goods return note raised to return with the goods if items are not appropriate.

(iv) The purchase order and related delivery documentation (delivery note or GRN) or copy goods return note should be sent to the accounts department to be matched to the invoice.

Note. Based on the information available at the time this book was written, we anticipate a task like this would be human marked in the real assessment.

Task 23

Helena Ltd has profit before tax of £140,000. The directors have included in trade receivables a debt of £9,000. The customer has recently gone into administration. There are no other uncorrected misstatements.	Qualified opinion – material misstatement
There was a flood at Douglas Ltd and several sales invoice files were destroyed. A copy of the sales invoice is matched with the goods despatched form and kept in the unaffected warehouse stores for 12 months.	Unmodified opinion only

BPP PRACTICE ASSESSMENT 2
EXTERNAL AUDITING

Time allowed: 2 hours

External Auditing: BPP practice assessment 2

Task 1

Which ONE of the following is a description of negative assurance?

	✓
A statement that nothing has come to the practitioner's attention to indicate that a true and fair view is not given	
A statement that the practitioner cannot tell whether a true and fair view is given due to insufficient evidence	
A statement that the practitioner feels a true and fair view is given	
A statement that the practitioner does not feel a true and fair view is given	

Task 2

Identify whether each of the following audit objectives is a legal requirement in the UK by selecting the appropriate option.

	Legal requirement ✓	Not a legal requirement ✓
Obtain reasonable assurance that the financial statements are free from material misstatement.		
Give an opinion as to whether the financial statements give a true and fair view.		
Maintain professional scepticism when planning and performing the audit.		

Task 3

Identify whether the following statements in respect of external auditor's liability limitation are true or false, by selecting the appropriate option.

Auditors can negotiate a limited liability agreement with clients so that they are not liable for damages above certain pre-agreed limits.	▼
Audit firms can function as Limited Liability Partnerships which means that partners' personal liability is restricted in the same way as a company shareholder's, but the audit firm may still be liable to clients for negligence.	▼

Picklist:

True
False

Task 4

(a) **Identify, for each of the descriptions below, the concept it represents.**

A member shall not make use of information obtained during the course of a business or professional relationship for personal gain.

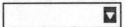

Picklist:

Confidentiality
Professional competence and due care

The avoidance of circumstances that a reasonable and informed third party would conclude as having compromised an individual's integrity, objectivity or professional scepticism.

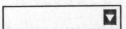

Picklist:

Independence in appearance
Objectivity

(b) **Which one of the following situations is likely to give rise to an advocacy threat to independence and objectivity?**

	✓
Concern about the possibility of losing a client	
Promoting shares in a listed entity when that entity is a financial statement audit client	
Being threatened with litigation in a court of law	

Task 5

Below are two statements regarding potential safeguards to be applied to protect an external auditor's independence and objectivity.

Identify whether each statement is true or false.

	True ✓	False ✓
Disciplinary procedures to ensure adherence to the AAT Code of Ethics		
Disclosure and discussion of ethical issues when performing both tax services and the external audit for the same client		

Task 6

During the audit of Clouds Ltd, the audit junior was asked by a senior member of staff if he could disclose to him the salary levels of other senior ranking members of staff.

Which ONE of the following is NOT an appropriate action for the audit junior to take?

	✓
Disclosing the information	
Discussing the matter with the audit senior before talking again to the senior staff member	
Reporting the matter to the audit partner directly	
Ringing the ethical helpline of his professional body for advice	

Task 7

(a) **Identify whether the following statements relating to the control environment of a company are true or false by selecting the appropriate option.**

If an auditor assesses that a control environment is strong, he must exercise professional scepticism.	▼
It is not possible for an individual to perpetrate a fraud when the control environment is strong and auditors exercise professional scepticism.	▼

Picklist:

True
False

(b) **Which ONE of the following is NOT a limitation of internal control systems?**

	✓
Human error in executing the controls	
Human error in designing the controls	
Collusion in circumventing the controls	
Lack of an internal audit function to monitor the controls	

Task 8

Accounting systems have control objectives and control procedures to mitigate the risks that the control objective is not met.

For each of the following, select whether they are a control objective, risk or control procedure.

Company pays the correct employees	▼
Company pays the incorrect employees	▼
Company checks pay against budgets	▼

Picklist:

Control objective
Control procedure
Risk

Task 9

External auditors use a variety of different types of working paper to ascertain systems.

(a)   Match the following descriptions to the type of working paper, using drag and drop from the pick list below.

A list of questions designed to give reasonable assurance of effective internal control within a given transactions cycle.	▼
A picture of the system using symbols with limited narrative.	▼
A list of controls expected to exist within a system.	▼

Picklist:

Audit strategy
Automated working paper
Checklist
Flowchart
ICQ
Narrative notes

The following are descriptions of procedures within the purchases system of Brunswick Ltd.

(b)   Identify whether each of the following procedures is a strength or a deficiency of that system by selecting the appropriate option.

John inspects all goods inwards, filing the delivery note in the production office. No other procedures are performed.	▼
Supplier statements are sent to Sandra, who reconciles them with the purchase ledger.	▼

Task 10

An entity uses internal control procedures in order to mitigate risks to which the entity is exposed. Listed below are two risks that exist in the sales system.

Match each internal control procedure with the risk it is designed to mitigate, by completing the table with the appropriate procedure for each risk.

Risk mitigated	Internal control procedure to mitigate
Customer has a poor credit rating	▼
Goods despatched but not invoiced	▼

Picklist:

Credit checks prior to accepting custom
Customer's existing balance checked prior to acceptance of order
Goods despatch notes matched with invoice
Goods outwards checked for quality

Task 11

Auditors use tests of control and substantive procedures to gather audit evidence.

Identify, for each of the following procedures, whether it is a test of control or a substantive procedure, by selecting the appropriate option.

	Test of control ✓	Substantive procedure ✓
Review of budgets prepared by the company		
Vouching of a payment listed on a bank reconciliation to the bank statement		
Observation of staff carrying out the inventory count		

Task 12

Identify whether each of the following statements, in respect of computer assisted audit techniques (CAATs) is true or false by selecting the appropriate option.

	True ✓	False ✓
Auditors can use CAATs to select samples.		
Auditors can use CAATs to test controls inherent in computer applications, for example, controls over invoices input to the sales ledger.		
Auditors should never input false invoices to a client's system when using CAATs.		

Task 13

When selecting items in order to perform audit tests, the auditor must ensure that every sampling unit in the population has a chance of being selected. There are some common methods of selecting a sample, described below.

Using the picklist, identify which method is described in each case.

The auditor uses a computer program or table to select the sample.	▼
The auditor uses a value-weighted selection.	▼
The auditor uses no structured technique.	▼

Picklist:

Haphazard selection
Interval sampling
Money Unit Sampling
Random numbers

Task 14

The external auditor may seek to place reliance on internal controls in order to restrict substantive testing.

Identify, in each of the following circumstances, whether the external auditor is likely or unlikely to place reliance on internal controls by selecting the appropriate option.

	Likely ✓	Unlikely ✓
Lizbet Ltd has been a client for two years. After the previous two audits, the firm raised control issues with the client in a report to management, and the recommendations were implemented. The directors are keen to improve the company's operations. The audit team has not relied on controls in the previous audits.		
Mattieu Ltd is a new client. An audit team has ascertained its controls system, which is extensive, and have been given access to the internal audit department's most recent report on controls.		
Emilie Ltd is an established client. The managing director is closely involved in all key aspects of the business and favours getting things done over following the book.		

Task 15

Auditors use a variety of procedures to test financial statement assertions.

From the descriptions below, using the picklist, identify the assertion being tested.

Reviewing a purchase invoice to confirm the purchase price of a non-current asset	▼
Tracing a sample of purchase invoices to authorised orders and goods received notes (GRNs)	▼

Picklist:

Accuracy, valuation and allocation
Completeness
Existence
Occurrence

Task 16

When planning an audit of financial statements, the external auditor is required to assess the risks of material misstatement arising in the financial statements.

(a)   Identify which component of audit risk the following represent by selecting the appropriate option.

The company has a high number of cash sales.	▼
A one-man operation has recently expanded and taken on staff, and the structures and operating practices have not yet been analysed and formalised.	▼
The directors all have profit-related bonuses.	▼

Picklist:

Control
Detection
Inherent

The external auditor assesses control risk in order to determine the audit approach.

(b)   Identify whether the following factors are likely to lead to the auditor assessing that there is an increase or a decrease in control risk by selecting the appropriate option.

The company has an internal audit function.	▼
The staff in the accounts department have all worked in their positions for a very long time.	▼
There is a new managing director at the company who is impatient of control restraints.	▼

Picklist:

Decrease
Increase

Kitchwood Ltd has had to respond to a new competitor in its market in the year to 31 March 20X5. Some extracts from the statement of profit and loss are as follows:

	20X5 £	20X4 £
Sales revenue	3,453,676	3,579,439
Advertising	31,885	23,689
	%	%
Gross margin	38	40

(c) **Which TWO of the following may provide a plausible explanation for movements in Kitchwood's statement of profit and loss?**

	✓
Increased spending on advertising has caused gross margin to fall.	
A high margin product became obsolete during the year.	
20X4 sales included a large one-off sale at a lower margin.	
There was a cut off error at the end of 20X4 and next year sales were included wrongly.	

Task 17

Which ONE of the following is a valid definition of materiality?

	✓
5% of profit before tax	
Measure of the significance of an item to readers	
Amount set by auditors as less than materiality for the whole financial statement	
Chance of the auditors drawing an incorrect audit conclusion	

Task 18

During the year, Bells Ltd built itself a new head office. The company took out a bank loan to finance the construction. Interest on the loan is charged at 3%. The company has retained a file of invoices relating to the construction. A specific labour team was used, and hours recorded on the job have also been recorded.

Required

Set out, in a manner suitable for inclusion in the audit plan:

(a) **The risks relating to the new head office, and**

(b) **The procedures to be undertaken to ensure that the building is properly valued in the financial statements.**

Task 19

You are planning the tests of detail over the payroll at Vance Ltd, to verify the assertions occurrence, measurement and completeness. The payroll is produced by Annie, who obtains monthly clockcards from the production manager, inputs the hours into her computer package which contains all the other relevant details from the employee files, and runs the payroll. It is taken to a director for approval before electronic payments are made to employees. Sample size has been set at six.

Required

Set out, in a manner suitable for inclusion in the audit plan, the audit tests to be carried out on payroll. You are not required to set out tests relating to leavers and joiners.

Task 20

Which of the following reasons audit working papers are prepared is the most important?

	✓
Assisting the audit team to plan and perform the audit	
Creating a record of the audit work carried out to support the audit opinion	
Retaining a record of matters of continuing significance	
Enabling external inspections if necessary (for example, by the FRC)	

Task 21

In each of the following situations, identify whether or not they should be referred to the audit supervisor.

Situation	Refer to supervisor ✓	Do not refer to supervisor ✓
During the audit of Birch Ltd, the audit junior identified that the owner-director of Fasterfoods Ltd, a supplier of foods to restaurants, often took goods home for his own use without noting what he had taken.		
During the audit of Rocksteady Ltd, the audit junior discovered two instances of the client staff misfiling sales invoices. He reviewed the records and found no evidence of the transactions having been input wrongly.		
Tombli Ltd has a large debt due from Boo Ltd, which the directors believe to be in doubt. The directors have informed the auditors that they believe this debt is not recoverable and have written down its value in the financial statements.		

Task 22

During the audit of Beaper Ltd, a new client, it was discovered that the company does not maintain inventory records. Peter Veales is in charge of inventory. He issues inventory to production staff when requested, and reorders when inventory seems low. Levels of inventory are monitored annually, when the company carries out its inventory count.

Required

Prepare extracts, suitable for inclusion in a report to management of Beaper Ltd, which set out:

(a) The possible consequences in respect of this matter, and
(b) The recommendations that you would make.

Task 23

For each of the following situations which have arisen in two unrelated audit clients, select whether or not the auditor's report on the financial statements would be modified.

Delta Ltd has a large debt due from Zeta Ltd, which the auditors believe to be in doubt. The directors disagree with the auditors, but have made the amendments in the financial statements the auditors believe necessary.	▼
During the year, Gamma Ltd has been involved in a court case, whose outcome is uncertain. An employee is suing the company for disability discrimination, and if his case were found in his favour, which the lawyers believe to be probable, the compensation could be material. The auditors believes a contingent liability should have been disclosed in the financial statements, but management refuse to disclose the contingent liability.	▼

Picklist:

Modified
Not modified

BPP PRACTICE ASSESSMENT 2
EXTERNAL AUDITING

ANSWERS

External Auditing: BPP practice assessment 2

Task 1

	✓
A statement that nothing has come to the practitioner's attention to indicate that a true and fair view is not given	✓
A statement that the practitioner cannot tell whether a true and fair view is given due to insufficient evidence	
A statement that the practitioner feels a true and fair view is given	
A statement that the practitioner does not feel a true and fair view is given	

Task 2

	Legal requirement ✓	Not a legal requirement ✓
Obtain reasonable assurance that the financial statements are free from material misstatement.		✓
Give an opinion as to whether the financial statements give a true and fair view.	✓	
Maintain professional scepticism when planning and performing the audit.		✓

(Giving an opinion in relation to a true and fair view is a UK legal requirement.)

Task 3

Auditors can negotiate a limited liability agreement with clients so that they are not liable for damages above certain pre-agreed limits.	True
Audit firms can function as Limited Liability Partnerships which means that partners' personal liability is restricted in the same way as a company shareholder's, but the audit firm may still be liable to clients for negligence.	True

Task 4

(a) A member shall not make use of information obtained during the course of a business or professional relationship for personal gain.

> Confidentiality

The avoidance of circumstances that a reasonable and informed third party would conclude as having compromised an individual's integrity, objectivity or professional scepticism.

> Independence in appearance

(b)

	✓
Concern about the possibility of losing a client	
Promoting shares in a listed entity when that entity is a financial statement audit client	✓
Being threatened with litigation in a court of law	

Task 5

	True ✓	False ✓
Disciplinary procedures to ensure adherence to the AAT Code of Ethics.	✓	
Disclosure and discussion of ethical issues when performing both tax services and the external audit for the same client.		✓ This is used in cases where there are relationships – such a threat is more likely to require separate teams.

Task 6

	✓
Disclosing the information	✓
Discussing the matter with the audit senior before talking again to the senior staff member	
Reporting the matter to the audit partner directly	
Ringing the ethical helpline of his professional body for advice	

It would be inappropriate for him to disclose this confidential information to the staff member. It would not be wrong for him to ring the ethical helpline, but it would probably be unnecessary – as it would be best for him to seek advice from other members of the audit team first.

Task 7

(a)

If an auditor assesses that a control environment is strong, he must exercise professional scepticism.	True
It is not possible for an individual to perpetrate a fraud when the control environment is strong and auditors exercise professional scepticism.	False

(b)

	✓
Human error in executing the controls	
Human error in designing the controls	
Collusion in circumventing the controls	
Lack of an internal audit function to monitor the controls	✓

Task 8

Company pays the correct employees	Control objective
Company pays the incorrect employees	Risk
Company checks pay against budgets	Control procedure

Task 9

(a)

A list of questions designed to give reasonable assurance of effective internal control within a given transactions cycle	ICQ
A picture of the system using symbols with limited narrative	Flowchart
A list of controls expected to exist within a system	Checklist

(b)

John inspects all goods inwards, filing the delivery note in the production office. No other procedures are performed.	Deficiency
Supplier statements are sent to Sandra, who reconciles them with the purchase ledger.	Strength

Task 10

Risk mitigated	Internal control procedure to mitigate
Customer has a poor credit rating	Credit checks prior to accepting custom
Goods despatched but not invoiced	Goods despatch notes matched with invoice

Task 11

	Test of control ✓	Substantive procedure ✓
Review of budgets prepared by the company	✓ – If the auditor were comparing to actual or to prior year budgets it might be a substantive procedure but in isolation it is a test that the control of preparing budgets exists.	
Vouching of a payment listed on a bank reconciliation to the bank statement		✓
Observation of staff carrying out the inventory count	✓	

Task 12

	True ✓	False ✓
Auditors can use CAATs to select samples.	✓	
Auditors can use CAATs to test controls inherent in computer applications, for example, controls over invoices input to the sales ledger.	✓	
Auditors should never input false invoices to a client's system when using CAATs.		✓

Task 13

The auditor uses a computer program or table to select the sample.	Random numbers
The auditor uses a value-weighted selection.	Money Unit Sampling
The auditor uses no structured technique.	Haphazard selection

Task 14

	Likely ✓	Unlikely ✓
Lizbet Ltd has been a client for two years. After the previous two audits, the firm raised control issues with the client in a report to management, and the recommendations were implemented. The directors are keen to improve the company's operations. The audit team has not relied on controls in the previous audits.	✓ – Reliance on controls is an efficient audit method. There is a good control environment and improved controls.	
Mattieu Ltd is a new client. An audit team has ascertained its controls system, which is extensive, and have been given access to the internal audit department's most recent report on controls.	✓ – There is a significant control system, and evidence of monitoring and improvement.	
Emilie Ltd is an established client. The managing director is closely involved in all key aspects of the business and favours getting things done over following the book.		✓ – Weak control environment.

Task 15

Reviewing a purchase invoice to confirm the purchase price of a non-current asset	Accuracy, valuation and allocation
Tracing a sample of purchase invoices to authorised orders and goods received notes (GRNs)	Occurrence – If you selected 'Existence' you treated these as assets, not expenses.

Task 16

(a)

The company has a high number of cash sales.	Inherent
A one-man operation has recently expanded and taken on staff, and the structures and operating practices have not yet been analysed and formalised.	Control
The directors all have profit-related bonuses.	Inherent

(b)

The company has an internal audit function.	Decrease
The staff in the accounts department have all worked in their positions for a very long time.	Decrease
There is a new managing director at the company who is impatient of control restraints.	Increase

(c)

	✓
Increased spending on advertising has caused gross margin to fall.	
A high margin product became obsolete during the year.	✓
20X4 sales included a large one-off sale at a lower margin.	
There was a cut off error at the end of 20X4 and next year sales were included wrongly.	✓

Task 17

	✓
5% of profit before tax	
Measure of the significance of an item to readers	✓
Amount set by auditors as less than materiality for the whole financial statement	
Chance of the auditors drawing an incorrect audit conclusion	

Task 18

(a) Risks

  (i) The building may not be valued correctly in the financial statements for various reasons:

   – Costs may have been omitted from the valuation.

   – Bank interest may have been omitted from the valuation or capitalised incorrectly.

   – The valuation might include elements of profit, that would usually be charged to customers.

(b) Procedures

  (i) Obtain the valuation calculation

  (ii) Verify material costs to invoices

  (iii) Verify labour costs to timesheets and payroll

  (iv) Ensure no element of profit included in these elements of cost

  (v) Review invoices allocated to valuation to ensure reasonable to capitalise these costs

  (vi) Verify capitalised bank interest to bank statements

Note. Based on the information available at the time this book was written, we anticipate a task like this would be human marked in the real assessment.

Task 19

Payroll

(1) Select six payroll entries from across the year (suggest one every two months)

(2) Confirm pay rates/tax rates/deductions to employee files

(3) Confirm hours worked to monthly clockcard

(4) Confirm calculations inherent in payroll (net pay, deductions, gross pay)

(5) Confirm deductions (NI, PAYE and any pension/other) have been made correctly

(6) Trace net pay to bank payment records

(7) Ensure payroll authorised by senior official

(8) Agree payment to bank statement/cash book

Note. Based on the information available at the time this book was written, we anticipate a task like this would be human marked in the real assessment.

Task 20

	✓
Assisting the audit team to plan and perform the audit	
Creating a record of the audit work carried out to support the audit opinion	✓
Retaining a record of matters of continuing significance	
Enabling external inspections if necessary (for example, by the FRC)	

Task 21

Situation	Refer to supervisor ✓	Do not refer to supervisor ✓
During the audit of Birch Ltd, the audit junior identified that the owner-director of Fasterfoods Ltd, a supplier of foods to restaurants, often took goods home for his own use without noting what he had taken.	✓	
During the audit of Rocksteady Ltd, the audit junior discovered two instances of the client staff misfiling sales invoices. He reviewed the records and found no evidence of the transactions having been input wrongly.		✓
Tombli Ltd has a large debt due from Boo Ltd, which the directors believe to be in doubt. The directors have informed the auditors that they believe this debt is not recoverable and have written down its value in the financial statements.		✓

Task 22

(a) Consequences

(i) Inventory is issued to production staff when requested, so there is a risk that inventory may be used inefficiently in production – with no records to show how much was used on a particular job there is no control over how efficiently the company operates.

(ii) As inventory is only monitored annually, it is at risk of being subject to theft – there is little to stop Peter defrauding the company by taking goods for personal use.

(iii) With no planning of the use of inventory, and Peter repurchasing when things seem low, there is a risk that goods will be unavailable when required for use in the business.

(b) Recommendations

(i) Inventory use should be better planned so that inventory is always available when required – re order levels should be set based on normal usage, and requisitions made when unusual usage is anticipated.

(ii) Inventory movements to production could be recorded, and possibly allocated to job number which records could be reviewed to ensure that inventory is used in an efficient manner.

Note. Based on the information available at the time this book was written, we anticipate a task like this would be human marked in the real assessment.

Task 23

Delta Ltd has a large debt due from Zeta Ltd, which the auditors believe to be in doubt. The directors disagree with the auditors, but have made the amendments in the financial statements the auditors believe necessary.	Not modified – As the directors have made the appropriate changes, the opinion will be unmodified.
During the year, Gamma Ltd has been involved in a court case, whose outcome is uncertain. An employee is suing the company for disability discrimination, and if his case were found in his favour, which the lawyers believe to be probable, the compensation could be material. The auditors believes a contingent liability should have been disclosed in the financial statements, but management refuse to disclose the contingent liability.	Modified – The lack of disclosure around the contingent liability will cause the audit opinion to be modified.

BPP PRACTICE ASSESSMENT 3
EXTERNAL AUDITING

Time allowed: 2 hours

External Auditing: BPP practice assessment 3

Task 1

Which ONE of the following is NOT a benefit of assurance?

	✓
Users of financial statements will have more confidence that they are presented fairly.	
Potential fraudsters might be deterred by regular scrutiny of the financial records.	
Management might be motivated to operate systems properly by the thought of a regular review of these systems.	
Investors will know the company is financially secure.	

Task 2

Complete the following statements on the regulation of auditors, by selecting the appropriate option in each case.

	True ✓	False ✓
Auditors should be independent of the company and its directors so that they can issue an objective opinion to the directors.		
Two-thirds of IAASB's board must approve a draft standard before it is issued as a new International Standard on Auditing.		
The IAASB is committed to seeking convergence between international and national standards on auditing to provide high quality auditing on a global basis.		

Task 3

Which ONE of the following is NOT a suitable way for auditors to limit their liability to their clients and other parties?

	✓
Disclaimer clause in the auditor's report	
Setting up a limited liability partnership	
Professional indemnity insurance	
Scrutinising every transaction entered by the business	

Task 4

(a) Identify, for each of the descriptions below, the threat it represents.

Independence can be threatened as the auditors can become over-reliant on the client, for instance, due to its fee income.

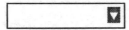

Picklist:

Self-interest
Self-review

Independence can be threatened if the auditors have prepared the financial statements being audited.

Picklist:

Intimidation
Self-review

(b) Which TWO of the following situations are definitions of the term 'professional behaviour'?

	✓
Avoiding any action that brings the profession into disrepute	
Maintaining professional knowledge and skill at the level required for an engagement	
Complying with relevant laws and regulations	

Task 5

Below are two statements regarding potential safeguards to be applied to protect an external auditor's independence and objectivity.

Identify whether each statement is true or false.

	True ✓	False ✓
Self-interest and intimidation threats from excessive fee dependency on one client can be overcome by consulting a third party on key points.		
Advocacy threats from family relationships with audit clients can be managed by removing the affected individual from the engagement team.		

Task 6

An audit senior has become involved in legal action related to some audit work he undertook on the audit of Seeker Ltd. The auditor has a duty of confidentiality to Seeker Ltd, but needs to defend himself against allegations that his work was not carried out with due care.

Which ONE of the following is not an appropriate action for the audit senior to take?

	✓
Maintain silence, so as not to breach confidentiality	
Obtain advice from his professional body concerning the matter	
Discuss the matter with his legal representation to obtain advice	
Disclose what work he did in respect of the matter, and risk breaching his duty of confidentiality	

Task 7

Identify whether the following statements in respect of limitations of internal controls are true or false, by selecting the appropriate option.

The fact that people using the system may make mistakes is not a limitation of internal controls.	▼
The fact that people may collude to override controls and commit a fraud is a limitation of internal controls.	▼
The fact that directors may omit important areas when designing control systems is not a limitation of internal controls.	▼

Picklist:

True
False

··

Task 8

Accounting systems have control objectives and control procedures to mitigate the risks that the control objective is not met.

Identify, for each of the following, whether they are a control objective, risk or control procedure, by selecting the appropriate option.

A company should only pay the correct suppliers.	▼
A company might pay a supplier twice for the same liability.	▼
A company should never allow blank cheques to be signed.	▼

Picklist:

Control objective
Control procedure
Risk

··

Task 9

An external auditor is required to obtain an understanding of the control environment within an audited entity.

(a) Identify whether the following factors contribute to a strong control environment or a weak control environment.

	Strong ✓	Weak ✓
The sales department is very target orientated. Staff and management are appraised solely on sales target achievements.		
The company has a dedicated internal audit department whose main role is to monitor adherence to company policies and procedures.		

External auditors use a variety of methods for documenting systems of control, including flowcharts, internal control questionnaires and narrative notes.

(b) For each of the following definitions, identify the method being described by selecting the appropriate method of documentation.

A list of questions designed to ascertain whether the system has a minimum level of controls to achieve objectives	▼
A description of the system	▼

Picklist:

Flowchart
Internal control questionnaire
Narrative notes

The following are descriptions of procedures within the non-current assets system of Primrose Ltd.

(c) **Identify whether each of the following procedures is a strength or a deficiency.**

	Strength ✓	Deficiency ✓
Divisional managers raise procurement orders for new non-current assets, which are approved by the board.		
Divisional managers are required to review all non-current assets in their divisions on a monthly basis.		

Task 10

An entity uses internal control procedures in order to mitigate the risks to which the entity is exposed. Listed below are two internal control procedures which are applicable to an entity's payroll system.

Identify, for each of the following internal control procedures, the risk that it mitigates, by completing the table with the risk mitigated.

Internal control procedure	Risk mitigated
Personnel records are kept and wages and salaries checked to details held in them.	▼
The payroll should be approved by someone who has not prepared it.	▼

Picklist:

A payroll fraud could be perpetrated
The bank may turn down the BACS request
The company may overpay its staff
The company might break the law relating to deductions

Task 11

Auditors use tests of control and substantive procedures to gather audit evidence.

Identify whether each of the procedures below is a test of control, an analytical procedure or a test of detail, by selecting the appropriate option.

The auditor is comparing the average salary per the payroll for last year to the average salary per the payroll for this year, taking into account known factors, such as the general 3% pay rise.	▼
The auditor is inspecting a purchase invoice for evidence that Doris, the purchase ledger clerk, checked the calculations on the invoice prior to entering the invoice into the system.	▼
The auditor is inspecting a purchase invoice to vouch the value of an addition to non-current assets.	▼

Picklist:

Analytical procedure
Test of control
Test of detail

Task 12

Select which Computer Assisted Audit Technique (CAAT) should be used in the following situations.

To help an auditor to select a sample from a large population	▼
To help an auditor compare large volumes of data from the current and prior year	▼
To help an auditor test whether application controls are working in a computer programme	▼

Picklist:

Audit software
Test data

Task 13

When selecting items in order to perform tests of detail, the auditor has to consider a number of factors.

Identify, for each of the following factors, the impact they will have on sample size by selecting the appropriate option.

Stratifying the sample by value	▼
Testing 100% of the population	▼
Decision to carry out initial analytical procedures on the population	▼

Picklist:

Decrease
Increase
No effect

Task 14

The external auditor may seek to place reliance on internal controls in order to restrict substantive testing.

Identify, in each of the following circumstances, whether the external auditor is likely to place reliance, or place no reliance on internal controls, by selecting the appropriate option.

The accounts department at Kadny Ltd consists of one member of staff.	▼
There is good segregation of duties at Tandy Ltd, and controls are monitored by management in each department.	▼
The controls at Landy Ltd sound good when described to the auditor, but they realise through observation that the financial controller regularly overrides controls to achieve objectives.	▼

Picklist:

No reliance
Reliance

Task 15

When testing transactions and balances, the external auditor will gain assurance about different assertions regarding those transactions and balances.

In respect of the assertions given below, select the information which will provide primary assurance.

Completeness of payables	▼
Valuation of raw materials	▼

Picklist: (Completeness of payables)

Purchase invoices
Supplier statements

Picklist: (Valuation of raw material)

Inventory records
Purchase invoice

Task 16

(a) Complete the following statements on the risk assessed by auditors by selecting the appropriate options.

(i) [▼] is the risk that the entity's internal control system will not prevent or detect and correct errors.

(ii) [▼] is the risk that misstatements will exist in financial statements and the auditors will not discover them.

(iii) [▼] is the risk that items will be misstated due to their nature or due to their context.

Picklist:

Audit risk
Control risk
Detection risk
Inherent risk

The external auditor assesses control risk in order to determine the audit approach.

(b) **Identify whether the following factors are likely to lead to the auditor assessing that there is an increase or a decrease in control risk, by selecting the appropriate option.**

The financial controller submits detailed budgets to the managing director and scrutinises variances from actual in detail.	▼
The company has a detailed set of control procedures which staff are required to follow.	▼
The directors ensure there is good segregation of duties at the company.	▼

Picklist:

Decrease
Increase

The external auditor is required to undertake analytical procedures as part of the planning process in order to identify the risk of misstatement of figures in the financial statements. The auditors have calculated that gross profit percentage has risen from last year, but the sales director has informed them there have been no significant changes in operations, sales levels or sales mix since last year.

(c) **Which TWO of the following may provide a plausible explanation for the rise in gross profit?**

	✓
Sales invoices relating to the next period may have been wrongly included in the current period.	
Sales invoices relating to the current period may have been wrongly included in the next period.	
Purchase invoices relating to the current period may have been wrongly included in the next period.	
Purchase invoices relating to the next period may have been wrongly included in the current period.	

Task 17

Identify whether the following misstatements are likely to be considered material or not material by external auditors.

	Material ✓	Not material ✓
A condition of Jocey Ltd's loan finance is that profits cover interest on the loans three times. The auditors have discovered a miscalculation in depreciation that increases depreciation by £2,000, dropping the interest cover to 2 times.		
During the audit of Kaseys Ltd, the auditors consider that an error equal to 5% of profit or more is material. The auditors have just confirmed that a debt of £20,000 owed by a customer is irrecoverable. Profit is £550,000. Audit procedures have not identified any other misstatements in the receivables balance, and risk assessment procedures during audit planning has determined that trade receivables is a low-risk area.		

Task 18

At 30 June 20X2, Benja Ltd had a trade receivable outstanding from Mina Ltd of £250,000. This is a material debt. Mina Ltd is a long standing customer who has had a history of late payment. The audit senior has performed analytical review on the receivable, and it is 5% higher than last year. Sales revenue to Mina Ltd has not increased in the year.

Required

Identify, for the purposes of the audit plan:

(a) **The audit risks relating to the overall receivables balance resulting from this outstanding receivable, and**

(b) **The procedures to be taken to ensure that the receivable from Mina Ltd is fairly stated in the financial statements.**

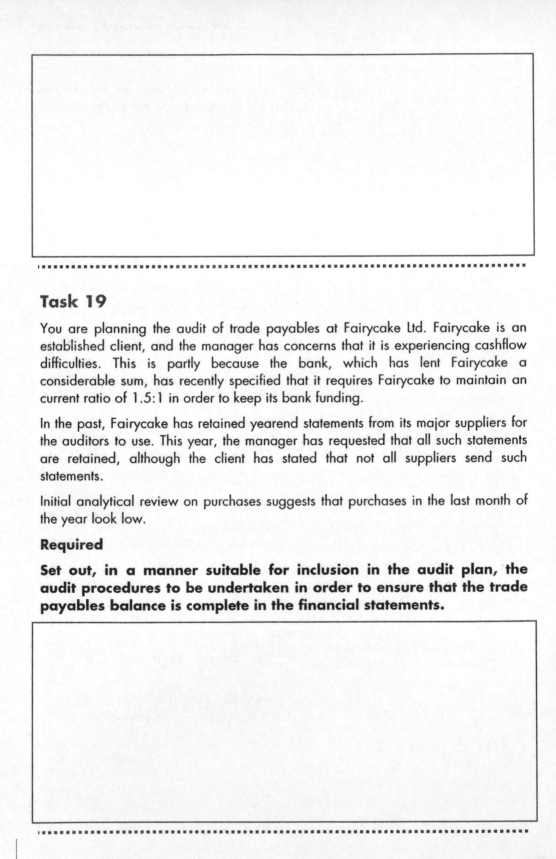

Task 19

You are planning the audit of trade payables at Fairycake Ltd. Fairycake is an established client, and the manager has concerns that it is experiencing cashflow difficulties. This is partly because the bank, which has lent Fairycake a considerable sum, has recently specified that it requires Fairycake to maintain an current ratio of 1.5:1 in order to keep its bank funding.

In the past, Fairycake has retained yearend statements from its major suppliers for the auditors to use. This year, the manager has requested that all such statements are retained, although the client has stated that not all suppliers send such statements.

Initial analytical review on purchases suggests that purchases in the last month of the year look low.

Required

Set out, in a manner suitable for inclusion in the audit plan, the audit procedures to be undertaken in order to ensure that the trade payables balance is complete in the financial statements.

BPP
LEARNING MEDIA

Task 20

Identify whether the following statements in respect of what will appear on an external auditor's working papers are true or false by selecting the appropriate option.

The date the work was carried out	▼
The date the work was reviewed by a more senior member of staff than the person who carried out the result	▼
The audit area being tested	▼

Picklist:

True
False

. . . .

Task 21

In each of the following situations, identify whether or not they should be referred to the audit supervisor.

Situation	Refer to supervisor ✓	Do not refer to supervisor ✓
During the audit of Crocus Ltd (annual revenue £12,000,000) for the year ended 31 December 20X1, when reviewing the cash book, the audit junior identified a monthly round sum payment of £1,000 to a company, entitled 'management charges'. Crocus is a single company with no other related companies.		
During the audit of Tulip Ltd, when reviewing the payroll, the audit junior noticed small number of staff had the same names as superhero characters (for example, Clark Kent and Peter Parker). He was suspicious of this, so requested their personnel files, which he was given. The files contain the same details as other personnel files he has seen. All of these staff work at the other site, which is a great distance from where the audit junior is based.		

Situation	Refer to supervisor ✓	Do not refer to supervisor ✓
The identification of a fraud, relating to an immaterial monetary amount, carried out by employee of the audited entity, due to a control deficiency previously communicated to management by the auditors.		

Task 22

During the audit of Daffs Ltd, a new client, the audit junior established that in the accounts department, Daphne records sales receipts with the receptionist. Daphne then posts receipts to the sales ledger, places the cheques in her desk drawer, which she locks when she is not at her desk. Receipts are all banked together on Friday afternoons.

Required

Prepare extracts, suitable for inclusion in a report to management of Daffs Ltd, which set out:

(a)   The possible consequences of this matter, and
(b)   The recommendations that you would make.

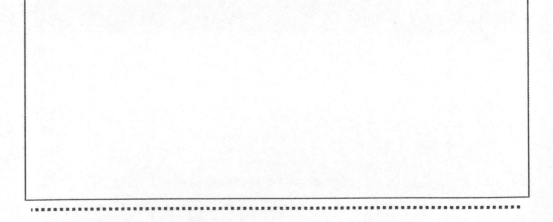

Task 23

For each of the following situations which have arisen in two unrelated audit clients, select whether or not the audit opinion on the financial statements would be modified.

The directors of Forsyth Ltd have included an optimistic value for a material investment in shares acquired in another company. The auditors believe that the value is incorrect and have asked for a more prudent amount to be included instead. The directors have refused.	▼
The directors at Jasmine Ltd prepared cash flow forecasts for the auditors to assess with regard to the going concern assumption. These forecasts covered a period of nine months after the year end. The directors refuse to extend the period of assessment. The auditors were not able to perform alternative procedures to verify the going concern assumption.	▼

Picklist:

Modified
Not modified

BPP PRACTICE ASSESSMENT 3 EXTERNAL AUDITING

ANSWERS

External Auditing: BPP practice assessment 3

Task 1

	✓
Users of financial statements will have more confidence that they are presented fairly.	
Potential fraudsters might be deterred by regular scrutiny of the financial records.	
Management might be motivated to operate systems properly by the thought of a regular review of these systems.	
Investors will know the company is financially secure.	✓

Task 2

	True ✓	False ✓
Auditors should be independent of the company and its directors so that they can issue an objective opinion to the directors.		✓ – The opinion is given to the shareholders
Two-thirds of IAASB's board must approve a draft standard before it is issued as a new International Standard on Auditing.	✓	
The IAASB is committed to seeking convergence between international and national standards on auditing to provide high quality auditing on a global basis.	✓	

Task 3

	✓
Disclaimer clause in the auditor's report	
Setting up a limited liability partnership	
Professional indemnity insurance	
Scrutinising every transaction entered by the business	✓

This would not guarantee a correct audit decision anyway, and would mean that the audit firm would surely go out of business, as their fees would be too high to compete with other firms.

....

Task 4

(a) Independence can be threatened as the auditors can become over-reliant on the client, for instance, due to its fee income.

> Self-interest

Independence can be threatened if the auditors have prepared the financial statements being audited.

> Self-review

(b)

	✓
Avoiding any action that brings the profession into disrepute.	✓
Maintaining professional knowledge and skill at the level required for an engagement.	– This is professional competence and due care.
Complying with relevant laws and regulations.	✓

....

Task 5

	True ✓	False ✓
Self-interest and intimidation threats from excessive fee dependency on one client can be overcome by consulting a third party on key points.	✓	
Advocacy threats from family relationships with audit clients can be managed by removing the affected individual from the engagement team.		✓ – Familiarity is the most likely threat here, not advocacy.

Task 6

	✓
Maintain silence, so as not to breach confidentiality	✓
Obtain advice from his professional body concerning the matter	
Discuss the matter with his legal representation to obtain advice	
Disclose what work he did in respect of the matter, and risk breaching his duty of confidentiality	

The auditor is entitled to defend himself in a legal situation. Seeking advice from his solicitor and professional body are also acceptable.

Task 7

The fact that people using the system may make mistakes is not a limitation of internal controls.	False
The fact that people may collude to override controls and commit a fraud is a limitation of internal controls.	True
The fact that directors may omit important areas when designing control systems is not a limitation of internal controls.	False

Task 8

A company should only pay the correct suppliers.	Control objective
A company might pay a supplier twice for the same liability.	Risk
A company should never allow blank cheques to be signed.	Control procedure

Task 9

(a)

	Strong ✓	Weak ✓
The sales department is very target orientated. Staff and management are appraised solely on sales target achievements.		✓
The company has a dedicated internal audit department whose main role is to monitor adherence to company policies and procedures.	✓	

(b)

A list of questions designed to ascertain whether the system has a minimum level of controls to achieve objectives	Internal control questionnaire
A description of the system	Narrative notes

(c)

	Strength ✓	Deficiency ✓
Divisional managers raise procurement orders for new non-current assets, which are approved by the board.	✓ – Purchases are authorised.	
Divisional managers are required to review all non-current assets in their divisions on a monthly basis.	✓ – The company ensures it assets are maintained properly.	

Task 10

Internal control procedure	Risk mitigated
Personnel records are kept and wages and salaries checked to details held in them.	The company may overpay its staff
The payroll should be approved by someone who has not prepared it.	A payroll fraud could be perpetrated

Task 11

The auditor is comparing the average salary per the payroll for last year to the average salary per the payroll for this year, taking into account known factors, such as the general 3% pay rise.	Analytical procedure
The auditor is inspecting a purchase invoice for evidence that Doris, the purchase ledger clerk, checked the calculations on the invoice prior to entering the invoice into the system.	Test of control
The auditor is inspecting a purchase invoice to vouch the value of an addition to non-current assets.	Test of detail

Task 12

To help an auditor to select a sample from a large population	Audit software
To help an auditor compare large volumes of data from the current and prior year	Audit software
To help an auditor test whether application controls are working in a computer programme	Test data

Task 13

Stratifying the sample by value	Decrease
Testing 100% of the population	Increase
Decision to carry out initial analytical procedures on the population	Decrease

Task 14

The accounts department at Kadny Ltd consists of one member of staff.	No reliance
There is good segregation of duties at Tandy Ltd, and controls are monitored by management in each department.	Reliance
The controls at Landy Ltd sound good when described to the auditor, but they realise through observation that the financial controller regularly overrides controls to achieve objectives.	No reliance

Task 15

Completeness of payables	Supplier statements
Valuation of raw materials	Purchase invoice

Task 16

(a)

(i) Control risk is the risk that the entity's internal control system will not prevent or detect and correct errors.

(ii) Detection risk is the risk that misstatements will exist in financial statements and the auditors will not discover them.

(iii) Inherent risk is the risk that items will be misstated due to their nature or due to their context.

(b)

The financial controller submits detailed budgets to the managing director and scrutinises variances from actual in detail.	Decrease
The company has a detailed set of control procedures which staff are required to follow.	Decrease
The directors ensure there is good segregation of duties at the company.	Decrease

(c)

	✓
Sales invoices relating to the next period may have been wrongly included in the current period.	✓
Sales invoices relating to the current period may have been wrongly included in the next period.	
Purchase invoices relating to the current period may have been wrongly included in the next period.	✓
Purchase invoices relating to the next period may have been wrongly included in the current period.	

Task 17

	Material ✓	Not material ✓
A condition of Jocey Ltd's loan finance is that profits cover interest on the loans three times. The auditors have discovered a miscalculation in depreciation that increases depreciation by £2,000, dropping the interest cover to 2 times.	✓	
During the audit of Kaseys Ltd, the auditors consider that an error equal to 5% of profit or more is material. The auditors have just confirmed that a debt of £20,000 owed by a customer is irrecoverable. Profit is £550,000. Audit procedures have not identified any other misstatements in the receivables balance, and risk assessment procedures during audit planning has determined that trade receivables is a low-risk area.		✓

Task 18

(a) **Audit risks**

(i)   There is a risk that the receivable contains an element which Mina Ltd does not intend, or can't afford, to pay.

(ii) There is a risk that Mina Ltd is in financial difficulties and the whole amount will become irrecoverable.

(b) **Procedures**

(i)   Request that the client seek confirmation from Mina Ltd that it intends to pay the balance (confirmation should be sent direct to auditors)

(ii) Scrutinise reply from Mina Ltd and draw audit conclusions about the recoverability of the balance

In addition, or instead if Mina Ltd does not reply after prompting:

(iii) Obtain an aged analysis of Mina's balance

(iv) Scrutinise aged analysis for any old balances that have not been paid, and analyse the payment pattern on the account (are older amounts paid in advance of newer invoices?)

(v)   Review payments after date (if any) and compare to age analysis

(vi) Discuss audit findings with credit controller to assess whether he has any relevant additional information about Mina's outstanding balance

Note. Based on the information available at the time this book was written, we anticipate a task like this would be human marked in the real assessment.

Task 19

(a)   Select a sample of payables balances to verify. As payables has been determined to be risky this year, this sample will be higher than in previous years. It should include all material items at the year end and a representative sample from the rest, perhaps selected systematically so as to avoid bias to high value items.

(b)   Obtain supplier statements for the sampled items, and reconcile the purchase ledger balances to the supplier statements. Particular attention should be paid to Invoices from the last month of the year, which Fairycake may have (wrongly) deferred into the next year.

(c) If supplier statements are not available for sampled items, consider whether alternative procedures provide sufficient evidence (such as scrutinising purchase invoices on the account). This will depend in part on the strength of purchase controls, and in part on the results of supplier statement reconciliations. If invoices appear to have been routinely deferred, it may be necessary to circularise suppliers from whom no statements are available.

(d) Perform a review of goods received notes in the last week of the year, and ensure that related invoices have been processed in the correct period. If it appears invoices have been deliberated deferred, this test may need to be extended to earlier in the month.

Note. Based on the information available at the time this book was written, we anticipate a task like this would be human marked in the real assessment.

Task 20

The date the work was carried out	True
The date the work was reviewed by a more senior member of staff than the person who carried out the result	True
The audit area being tested	True

Task 21

Situation	Refer to supervisor ✓	Do not refer to supervisor ✓
During the audit of Crocus Ltd (annual revenue £12,000,000) for the year ended 31 December 20X1, when reviewing the cash book, the audit junior identified a monthly round sum payment of £1,000 to a company, entitled 'management charges'. Crocus is a single company with no other related companies.	✓ – Although the total amount transferred is immaterial, it is a round sum payment that has no obvious rationale – why would an unconnected company be paying management charges?	
During the audit of Tulip Ltd, when reviewing the payroll, the audit junior noticed small number of staff had the same names as superhero characters (for example, Clark Kent and Peter Parker). He was suspicious of this, so requested their personnel files, which he was given. The files contain the same details as other personnel files he has seen. All of these staff work at the other site, which is a great distance from where the audit junior is based	✓ – This could be legitimate, but could also be a payroll fraud, in which case the personnel files could have been invented as well. The supervisor might deem it necessary to identify one of the staff members at the other site, particularly if the sums involved for the superheroes salaries is material.	
The identification of a fraud, relating to an immaterial monetary amount, carried out by employee of the audited entity, due to a control deficiency previously communicated to management by the auditors.	✓ – This is could be a case of collusion and should be reported.	

Task 22

(a) **Consequences**

(i) Daphne's desk drawer does not seem to be a suitably secure place to store cash receipts, even if it sometimes locked. There is a significant risk that these receipts could be stolen or lost. In an extreme case, if the desk was affected by fire, the desk drawer is unlikely to be fireproof, and the cheques could be destroyed.

(ii) Receipts are only banked once a week, which exposes the company to the threat of their loss, and also the loss of potential interest on those receipts for the days that the receipts are owned but not cashed, or the lack of cash powering the business because it is in a desk drawer.

(b) **Recommendations**

(i) The company should invest in a safe so that receipts can be kept more securely when they have not yet been banked.

(ii) Daphne should bank receipts more frequently, ideally daily, which would convert the cheques to cash more quickly and also reduce the risk of loss.

(iii) In the long term, Daffs should consider asking customers to pay their balances by electronic transfer direct to their bank account, which would speed up the process of cash conversion further, and would eliminate the risk of loss of cash receipts.

Note. Based on the information available at the time this book was written, we anticipate a task like this would be human marked in the real assessment.

Task 23

The directors of Forsyth Ltd have included an optimistic value for a material investment in shares acquired in another company. The auditors believe that the value is incorrect and have asked for a more prudent amount to be included instead. The directors have refused.	**Modified** – The auditors cannot state that the financial statements contain a true and fair view of this material amount.
The directors at Jasmine Ltd prepared cash flow forecasts for the auditors to assess with regard to the going concern assumption. These forecasts covered a period of nine months after the year end. The directors refuse to extend the period of assessment. The auditors were not able to perform alternative procedures to verify the going concern assumption.	**Modified** – This leads to an inability to obtain sufficient appropriate audit evidence, as the auditors would expect to review going concern assessments covering at least 12 months.

103532

BPP
LEARNING MEDIA